Everything You Need to Know About Teaching But Are Too Busy to Ask

Everything You Need to Know About Teaching But Are Too Busy to Ask

Essential Briefings for Teachers

Brin Best and Will Thomas

continuum

Continuum International Publishing Group

The Tower Building   80 Maiden Lane, Suite 704

11 York Road   New York, NY 10038

London

SE1 7NX

www.continuumbooks.com

British Library Cataloguing-in-Publication Data

A catalogue record for this book is available from the British Library.

ISBN: 9780826483775 (paperback)

Library of Congress Cataloging-in-Publication Data

Best, Brin.

  Everything you need to know about teaching but are too busy to ask : essential briefings for teachers / Brin Best and Will Thomas.

    p. cm.

  Includes bibliographical references.

  ISBN-13: 978-0-8264-8377-5 (pbk.)

  ISBN-10: 0-8264-8377-1 (pbk.)

  1. Teaching--Terminology. I. Thomas, Will, 1968- II. Title.

  LB1025.3.B475 2007

  371.10203–dc22

                       2007026980

Typeset by Ben Cracknell Studios | www.benstudios.co.uk

Printed and bound in Great Britain by MPG Books Ltd, Bodmin

Contents

The briefings are listed alphabetically in tabular form below, showing how their content links with the *Five Domains of Effective Teaching* – see page 2 for details.

Acknowledgements

We would like to thank Alexandra Webster, publisher at Continuum, who first suggested that a book of briefings for teachers in this format might be welcomed by the profession. Her continued faith in us has been a constant source of encouragement throughout the project.

Gill O'Donnell made an important contribution to the book through researching several entries and also proofreading the whole work at various stages. Her ability to maintain meticulously high standards of proofreading, combined with an uncanny eye for what needs to be added from an educational standpoint, is deeply impressive. We thank her warmly for her efforts, while taking full responsibility for any errors which may remain.

As ever our families and friends have been a huge source of support as we worked on another book project together. Only they know how much they have contributed to our work.

Introduction

Everything You Need To Know About Teaching But Are Too Busy To Ask aims to lighten the load by fast-tracking you to essential information about the key issues underpinning your work as a teacher. We have brought together in this book 50 briefings which present, in a concise and jargon-free manner, what you need to know and how you can benefit from this information in your classroom. The briefings provide a knowledge base for some of the major contemporary themes in education, which can dovetail with your existing teaching knowledge and skills, gained from your training and experience to date. The content included here is free of political bias or spin and gets to the heart of the issues in question – though we do not shy away from expressing our own views on the topics covered.

This book can be seen as a companion volume to our *Creative Teaching and Learning Toolkit* (Continuum International Publishing, 2007), which set out a holistic framework outlining what constitutes effective teaching and learning. The basis of that framework consists of the *Five Domains of Effective Teaching*, namely:

- Vision
- Climate for learning
- Teaching and learning strategies
- Reflection
- Teachers' personal and professional domain

We use these domains in this book as a way of signalling the kind of information, skills and ideas covered in each of the briefings – this is presented in the contents page in tabular form. This also allows readers to carry out some targeting reading about specific domains, should they wish to do so. More extensive information and theoretical background on each of these domains is included in the *Creative Teaching and Learning Toolkit.*

The book is not meant to be read in one sitting and instead should be regarded as a document to be dipped into when the need arises. However, we have provided some structure to the organization of entries to help you navigate your way through the book and see how related entries in other sections and briefings might also be useful. Each entry follows a consistent format, as outlined below:

What is it?/What are they?

Here we present definitions of key terms mentioned, clarifying what is meant in an education context.

Knowledge bank

In this main section we outline in bullet point form the vital information about the topic. Our aim here is not to be completely exhaustive in our treatment, rather to summarize the salient points from the raft of information which has been published on the topic. Throughout this section we stress the information the classroom teacher needs to know. We also include best practice advice gathered from successful schools, with the hope that you can gain relevant knowledge and skills from other colleagues.

Ask yourself

For each briefing we provide a set of questions which should help you take things one step further – by reflecting on the content in the 'knowledge bank' and by considering your current practice in this area.

✓ To do list

We wish to make this book developmental by including suggested actions that will enable you to make improvements in as many areas as you wish. You can readily tailor your own CPD (continuing professional development) programme by focusing on those topics which are most relevant to your circumstances, or the challenges you're facing right now.

Want to find out more?

We are sure that you will wish to study in more detail some of the topics included in the book. For this reason at the end of each entry we include suggested further reading and information, including selected websites.

See also ...

This final part of the entry signposts you to other briefings in the book which are related to the one you're currently reading. As well as helping you to learn about associated topics, this aspect of the briefings is also intended to provide a springboard for you to browse through other entries.

Inevitably, some topics are covered in more depth than others, usually because the issues are more complex or broader in their scope. We also have dealt with those topics that especially interest us more comprehensively. As such, the length of the briefings should not necessarily be taken as being indicative of the relative importance of the topic covered – and in any case we are not trying to produce 'the last word' on these topics, rather to cover the more important ground so you can gain a firm grounding across the spectrum of topics covered.

Remember that the process of professional development is about recognizing where you currently are and working towards where you want to be. Some of the topics in this book will already be familiar to you; others will be hazy and a few may be new. If you identify first what you need to know and do in order to be more effective you can select readings from the book to help you to get there.

The book is linked to a continually updated website, where we will post new entries and provide updates to existing ones. We would, therefore, be interested to hear from you with suggested topics you would like to see covered. Please contact us via the website at www.creativityforlearning.co.uk.

Accelerated learning

What is it?

Accelerated learning is a set of principles and approaches to promoting effective learning. It rests on a foundation of neuro-scientific research from which is extrapolated a series of models and strategies that enhance the capacity of learners.

Knowledge bank

- Accelerated learning has a number of underpinning principles:
  - A focus on learning
  - A positive and purposeful learning environment
  - Connection to other learners
  - A cyclical approach to learning
  - Awareness of the styles and preference for learning that exist amongst learners.
- It makes use of *neuro-scientific research* to inform classroom practice. In particular, it draws on research from functional

scanning techniques about how the brain responds to learning tasks.

- There has been some criticism of accelerated learning for drawing broad general rules about learning in classrooms from discrete laboratory experiments, sometimes involving animals other than humans. This has been countered by case studies from teachers and schools using it to effect positive change in schools.
- Accelerated learning draws broad inferences about how we should plan for learning with the brain in mind, and although there is a range of interpretations of accelerated learning in the UK, a *cyclical process* is suggested by each proponent.
- The approach favoured by the authors is Alistair Smith's four-stage cycle consisting of:
- *Connection* (connecting learners to what they already know, to the content, the process of the learning and with one another)
- *Activation* (offering new ideas, concepts and activating thinking through a rich sensory immersion)
- *Demonstration* (the opportunity to show what has been learnt, to gain feedback and to practise skills, techniques and knowledge)
- *Consolidation* (the opportunity to review learning, and review how learning has taken place, to use techniques to commit learning to long-term memory and to consider ways in which learning could be transferred to other areas of school or home life).
- It incorporates models of thinking which both explain levels of cognitive challenge and also provide methodology to extend levels of thinking. Bloom's taxonomy of thinking is used as a framework to encourage six different types of thinking. These include knowledge recall, comprehension, application of learning, analysis, evaluation, and synthesis (or creative development of ideas).
- Accelerated learning provides a number of useful ways to think about the classroom and learners including:
  - The notion that intelligence is varied and modifiable, drawing on Howard Gardner's Multiple Intelligence Theory.
  - If we take care of the self-esteem and motivation, the behaviour will take care of itself. Accelerated learning draws on six elements of self-esteem which can be developed in classrooms using a range of strategies.

- All learners have different needs including sensory preferences
- There are no mistakes, only learning, which enables learners to take risks in their learning without fear of ridicule or derision.
- Classrooms are places of improvement not comparison, which puts an emphasis on self-motivation and improvement rather than a league table approach to success.

• Tools and strategies for promoting motivation, self-esteem, varietal thinking and memory are all included under the accelerated learning umbrella. These include a raft of memory improvement techniques and an education of learners about how their memory is organized and how they can improve it using memory techniques.

Ask yourself

1 How much are you currently utilizing research about the brain to inform your teaching?

2 What are the principles you're currently operating on in your classroom and how do they compare with those outlined for accelerated learning?

3 How much do you understand about the cyclical process of learning?

✓ To do list

☐ Consider reading more about brain function and its relationship to learning.

☐ Share what you know about brain function and learning with your learners.

☐ Consider being even more explicit with your learners about the principles upon which you operate your classroom.

☐ Read a book on accelerated learning within the next three months.

Want to find out more?

Best, B. (2003) *Accelerated Learning Pocketbook*. Teachers' Pocketbooks.

Hughes, M. (2001) *Closing the Learning Gap*. Network Educational Press.

Jensen, E. (1995) *Super Teaching*. The Brain Store Inc.

Lovatt, M. & Wise, D. (2001) *Creating an Accelerated Learning School*. Network Educational Press.

Smith, A. (2000) *Accelerated Learning in Practice*. Network Educational Press.

Information and training in Accelerated Learning (www.alite.co.uk)
- Comprehensive information on accelerated learning, including information on training. The site contains numerous case studies from schools using the approaches.

Specialist brain-based Learning Publisher (www.newhorizons.org)
- Lots of resources to enable you to find out more about brain-based approaches to learning.

Brain Connections Website (www.brainconnections.com)
- Excellent site with lots of information about brain research and its relevance to learning and health.

Brainstore Website (www.brainstore.com)
- Useful site with many resources and downloads on matters relating to accelerated learning. This is the site of Eric Jensen, a world leader in the subject.

See also . . .

→✣ Active learning, page 91.

→✣ Evidence-based teaching, page 57.

→✣ Neuro-linguistic programming, page 136.

→✣ Research in education, page 159.

2

Active learning

What is it?

Active learning centres on the process of learning through active *participation* in the classroom, field, in the workplace, in the community and in laboratories. Through activities which are as real as possible to the actual application of the ideas, learners are encouraged to come up with their own theoretical models and interpretations. Another definition of active learning is 'involving students in practising important skills and applying new knowledge' (John Hattie; see below).

Knowledge bank

- Research suggests that active participation in learning as against passive listening is more enjoyable, more memorable and more effectively understood.
- Active approaches to learning stimulate the brain to make neural *connections* (build synaptic links between brain cells) and it is this

connection which constitutes learning. It seems that passive listening approaches to learning are less effective at assisting us to make connections.

- Active learning lessons usually contain a number of similar features:
  - reviewing prior knowledge and understanding
  - demonstration by the teacher of how to do something or verbal introduction to important ideas
  - monitored practice where learners try the new skill or work with the new knowledge, with reflection on process as well as content
  - learners having opportunities to practise the skills or use the knowledge again on their own
  - extension assignments, e.g. for homework
  - further review to consolidate.
- Studies using control groups and test groups carried out by John Hattie showed that learners involved in an active learning process performed, on average, one and a half grades better than those taught with didactic, passive, teacher talk methods. In these studies, both groups were taught for the same amount of time.
- Active learning is based on a *constructivist* view of learning (→❖ **Constructivism**, page 27), that is, it sees learning as a building process where new meaning is made by reflecting on experience and relating this to existing meaning. Reflection is stimulated through meaningful practical experiences close to the application of the knowledge or skill. This means that concepts are not understood until it has been related to existing ideas, contexts, knowledge and skills.
- Active learning supports the 'making of meaning' and in this sense it enables learners to 'transform what is fragmentary or in separate compartments into a coherent whole' (Best *et al.* 2005).
- The activities involved in the active learning process must stimulate individuals to *question* their existing constructs, that is they need to encourage learners to question the concepts and connections they make between them. There is also a need for a period of reflection, where the ideas and experiences are explained to others, to themselves and to their teachers, so that new thinking can be affirmed and improved. Teaching others their new knowledge would seem to be the most effective method of ensuring recall over time.

Ask yourself

1 To what extent are your lessons active learning experiences?

2 How do you structure a learning period currently and what might you consider changing in the light of reading this briefing?

3 How are learners given opportunities for active reflection and interpersonal communication in your lessons?

4 Where does active learning happen and where does it not happen? What are the reasons for this?

✓ To do list

☐ Set up an audit of active learning in your classroom. Invite learners to score their levels of satisfaction from 1–10 in your lessons, comparing active lessons versus more didactic lessons. Ask them also to rate their understanding on the same 1–10 scale. Compare the results over a half term.

☐ Set up your own control study between different groups of learners and explore the differences over a module. Note that if you see key differences in performance, ethically you should cease your studies and go with the findings!

☐ Collect ideas from colleagues for active learning activities at the start of staff meetings or in informal discussions.

☐ Make reflection on active learning approaches a focus of lesson observations for professional development.

Want to find out more?

Best, B., Blake, A. & Varney, J. (2005) *Making Meaning: Learning Through Logovisual Thinking*. Chris Kington Publishing.

Hattie, J.A. *Influences on Student Learning*. This can be downloaded from Professor John Hattie's staff home page: www.arts.auckland.ac.nz/staff/index.cfm?P=5049

Muijs, D. & Reynolds, D. (2005) *Effective Teaching: Evidence and Practice*. Paul Chapman Publishing.

Petty, G. (2004) *Teaching Today: A Practical Guide*. Nelson Thornes.

Geoff Petty's website has been most informative in writing this briefing and provides further information on this topic at www.geoffpetty.com

An interesting college site promoting active learning approaches is The Centre for Active Learning at www.glos.ac.uk.

See also . . .

→❖ Accelerated learning, page 51.

→❖ Cognitive acceleration programmes, page 24.

→❖ Constructivism, page 27.

→❖ Enquiry-based learning, page 50.

→❖ Evidence-based teaching, page 57.

→❖ Teaching style, page 175.

3

Assessment for Learning

What is it?

Assessment for Learning (AfL) means using evidence and dialogue to identify where learners are in their learning, where they need to go and how best to get there. This means looking at evidence collaboratively, enabling learners to be clear what they need to do to improve and joining up learning and lesson planning processes.

Knowledge bank

- Some of the most well-known work done on Assessment for Learning was carried out by Paul Black and Dylan Wiliam. It is actually the drawing together of a large number of studies done worldwide, which provided evidence of improvement in attainment through *formative assessment* processes.
- A two-year research project carried out in Medway, Oxfordshire, provided further evidence of success in a UK setting. It is now

seen as a major plank in the government's drive to personalize education (→❖ **Personalization in education**, page 146).

- Black and Wiliam encouraged teachers to replace purely summative feedback (i.e. solely with the purpose of determining the performance of the learner) with feedback within the context of supporting improvement and development, where the learner is at the centre of the process.
- Assessment for Learning highlighted four key areas for transforming formative assessment in classrooms, these are:
  - *Questioning* – this includes putting more thought into framing high quality open questions which promote higher order thinking and increasing the amount of time learners have to think before answering.
  - *Feedback through marking* – where teachers encourage learners to expand upon and show understanding of what they have learnt. →❖ **Marking**, page 107.
  - *Peer and self-assessment using shared criteria* – where learners know what success looks like, and are taught the skills and attitudes of feedback and self-evaluation. Clear aims are required throughout so that learners can check back to see if they are meeting them.
  - *The formative use of summative tests* – where learners are engaged in reflective activities to review their work and prepare appropriate strategies. They also suggest that learners should be engaged in the process of setting and answering questions about the learning they have experienced. They should also be able to apply criteria to understand how they could improve in future.
- The *Assessment Reform Group* (ARG) was set up to bring research evidence about Assessment for Learning to the attention of education professionals, and based on the work of Black and Wiliam they have produced a series of ten principles for operating this formative approach in classrooms. These are:
  - Assessment for Learning should be part of effective planning of lessons where the teacher should plan how learners will receive feedback within the lesson.
  - It should focus on how learners learn. In both planning and learning learners should be encouraged to reflect on the 'how' of the learning process.

- It should be recognized as essential to classroom practice. The ARG recognizes that much of what learners and teachers do is about assessment and that learners should be involved in the decisions that are made.
- It should be recognized as a key professional tool for teachers. Teachers need to be supported in developing the skills of feedback and assessment.
- It should be sensitive and constructive, because all assessment has an emotional impact. An awareness of the impact of the assessment process is essential and feedback should be sensitively handled.
- Assessment should take account of learner motivation. Assessment which focuses on achievement rather than failure and that which provides learner choice and autonomy is encouraged.
- It should promote commitment to goals and a shared understanding of assessment criteria. The sharing of assessment criteria, enabling discussion about them, and in language that learners can understand is essential.
- Learners should receive constructive guidance about how they can improve. A focus on strengths for further improving successes and a sensitive addressing of weakness, with constructive guidance on how to improve, is necessary.
- It develops learners' capacity for self-assessment so that they become reflective and self-managing. It does this through encouraging the desire and promoting the development of the skills of self-assessment.
- It should recognize the full range of achievements of learners and be an inclusive process, aimed at engaging and supporting every learner's needs.

Ask yourself

1 How are you currently using Assessment for Learning approaches in your lessons? What might be your next steps?
2 How does Assessment for Learning build on what you already know and do in the classroom? How much of it is really 'new'?

3 What opportunities are there for sharing good practice with colleagues in this area?

✓ To do list

- ☐ Using the ten principles as an audit tool, rate your current level of practice for each. Use a 1–5 scale, where 1 is not at all and 5 is consistent.
- ☐ Having carried out the audit above, consider these questions: What are your strengths in relation to Assessment for Learning? What area would you most like to change? What might be the next step in changing this area?
- ☐ Ask your learners what their experiences are of the assessment process in your lessons. In particular pay attention to the usefulness of feedback for improvement and the emotional impact of different aspects of assessment.

Want to find out more?

Black, P. & Wiliam, D. (1998) *Inside the Black Box*. Kings College.

Black, P. & Wiliam, D. (2002) *Working inside the Black Box*. Kings College.

Black, P., Harrison, C., Lee, C., Marshall, B. & Wiliam, D. (2003) *Assessment for Learning: putting it into practice*. Open University Press.

Web address for the Assessment Reform Group: www.assessment-reform-group.org.uk/

Web address for the Assessment Reform Group Assessment for Learning Leaflet on the ten principles: www.aaia.org.uk/pdf/AFL_10principlesARG.pdf

See also . . .

→✤ Marking, page 107.

→✤ Target-setting approaches, page 172.

Brain breaks

What are they?

Brain breaks are pauses in learning taken in order to carry out physical activities for the purposes of enhancing learning. They can be set within a philosophy of a healthy lifestyle for effective learning.

Knowledge bank

- There are many commercially branded brain break activities which claim specific brain-related benefits. In some cases these brain break regimes include reference to the importance of nutrition and hydration in learning, and a quest to educate young people about the benefits of proper nutrition and hydration, sleep, exercise and laughter.
- Brain break activities are said to influence a range of aspects of learning and development including:
  - overall improvement in balance and coordination

- integration of the brain's function between the so-called left and right hemispheres of the brain, via the brain structure the *corpus callosum*
- improvement in attention through physical, intellectual and emotional reprieve; taking a break from your learning improves your concentration
- enhanced cardiovascular and respiratory function
- stress relief.

- Caution needs to be exercised in promoting some of the proposed benefits, as much of the science behind the claims has not yet been properly evidenced. However, many teachers report a range of *benefits* in their learners as a result of introducing brain break activities.

- Some proponents of brain break activities make claims that their approach has particular benefits for young people with dyslexia, dyspraxia and ADHD (Attention Deficit Hyperactivity Disorder).

- One approach advocated by Alistair Smith in *Move It* (2002) identifies eight different categories of movement:
  - relaxers to support emotional awareness of relaxation and anxiety
  - energizers to lift the energy levels of a group
  - stretchers to improve physical flexibility
  - lateralizers to assist children to develop a sense of left and right and to support coordination and balance
  - little and large movements to improve hand-eye coordination and voluntary muscle movements
  - coordinates done with other people in partnership, developing observation skills, mental rehearsal and cooperation
  - linkers to link directly with learning and content
  - eye trackers designed to improve eye movement tracking in relation to reading.

- Two examples of a brain break activity are:
  - *Cross crawl* – it is claimed that this helps to improve coordination and balance and is also a useful energizer activity. Stand with your feet shoulder width apart, once you are stable in your stance, lift your right knee and move your left hand across to touch it. Bring the knee down and the hand back to your side then repeat with the right hand and left knee. This should be repeated with each side 10–12 times.

– *Active punctuation* – designed to assist learners to learn content in the lesson. It consists of a series of movements to represent different aspects of punctuation, e.g. a small jump for a full stop, two hands in the air inclined to the left to start speech. These actions are added to prose as it is read out.

Ask yourself

1 How much movement do your learners currently enjoy in lessons?
2 What might be the benefits of learners having more structured movement in lessons?
3 How could you bring movement into lessons safely?
4 What else do you need to know or experience to take this further?

✓ To do list

☐ Read a good book or visit a website on educational kinesiology, brain breaks or Brain Gym®.

☐ Experiment safely with what you find out with a group of learners with whom you have a good relationship.

☐ Trial a range of brain break activities at different times of the day, and with different groups, and get feedback from learners using a question like: 'What were the benefits of the exercise?'

☐ Encourage learners to research the impact of diet, hydration, sleep and exercise on learning and to share their discoveries with the class.

Want to find out more?

Dennison, P. (1992) *Brain Gym*. Edu-Kinesthetics Inc.
Smith, A. (2002) *Move It: Physical Movement and Learning*. Network Educational Press.
Visit the website of Alastair Smith's company at www.alite.co.uk
Visit the Brain Gym® website at www.braingym.org.uk/ for further information and research.

See also . . .

→✧ Accelerated learning, page 5.
→✧ Differentiation, page 38.
→✧ Drama across the curriculum, page 42.
→✧ Managing learners' behaviour, page 95.
→✧ Teaching style, page 175.

5

Coaching

What is it?

Coaching is a relationship and a process which facilitates the learning of another.

Knowledge bank

- Coaching enables people to get unstuck when they reach blocks to their peak performance. It has variously been described as 'The purest form of personalized learning', 'Emotional Intelligence in Action' and 'Facilitating the learning and development of another'.
- Coaching differs from →❖ **Mentoring** (page 110) because it does not offer specific advice or guidance, but instead promotes the generation of personalized performance-enhancing solutions. It is focused on self-developed solutions and characterized by individuals learning through logic and trial and error so that they understand the process by which solutions are arrived at.

- Coaches operate on 10 key principles:
  - be non-judgemental
  - be non-critical
  - believe that people have the answers to their challenges within them
  - respect a person's confidentiality (as defined by the law)
  - be positive and believe there are always solutions to issues
  - pay attention to recognizing and pointing out strengths and build self-esteem
  - challenge individuals to move beyond their comfort zone
  - break down big goals into manageable steps
  - believe that self-knowledge improves performance
  - maintain a genuine willingness to learn from those you coach.
- Coaching involves the use of specific questioning techniques, effective listening skills and a simple problem-solving structure. One such example of a problem-solving structure is the STRIDE model. This invites you to focus on your *Strengths* to build resourceful thinking, to formulate a *Target* to bring direction to the discussion, to explore the *Reality*, so that you uncover what is stopping you from achieving your target. An *Ideas* step involves creatively looking at how you could meet your target and the *Decision* phase is the process of committing to a course of action. Finally, we *Evaluate* the action taken in a subsequent coaching conversation.
- It is an invaluable tool for managing people of all ages because it empowers them to generate appropriate solutions, allows them to generate repeatable performances and frees leaders from the high dependency relationships that can sometimes develop with others.
- Coaching can be used with learners and staff in schools in equal measure – it is gaining in popularity as a means of helping learners to reach their potential.

Ask yourself

1 To what extent are you currently using coaching in your lessons, and in other aspects of your work?
2 What might coaching have to offer you and your learners?

3 Consider any reasons why you have not yet engaged with coaching. What are these and are they really good reasons not to engage?

✓ To do list

☐ Read a good coaching text to find out more.

☐ Consider taking a course in coaching skills. Many one-day programmes exist that give you sufficient grounding in coaching to use it in your everyday work. Visit www.visionforlearning.co.uk and www.alite.co.uk for high quality coach training.

☐ Pay attention to the kinds of questions you ask of people at work. What proportion of them are open questions and what proportion are closed? Coaches ask a high proportion of open questions to promote deeper thinking.

Want to find out more?

McLeod, A. (2003) *Performance Coaching*. Crown House Publishing.

Thomas, W. & Smith, A. (2004) *Coaching Solutions: Practical Ways to Improve Performance in Education*. Network Educational Press.

Zeus, P. & Skiffington, S. (2002) *The Coaching at Work Toolkit*. McGraw-Hill.

Visit the website of Vision for Learning: www.visionforlearning.co.uk

Visit the website of The Institute of Educational Coaching: www.instituteofeducationalcoaching.co.uk

See also . . .

→❖ Mentoring, page 110.

→❖ Neuro-linguistic programming, page 136.

→❖ Personalization in education, page 146.

6

Cognitive acceleration programmes

What are they?

Cognitive acceleration programmes are intervention approaches which seek to enhance learning through the use of innovative methods centring on thinking skills.

Knowledge bank

- Cognitive acceleration programmes first came to the attention of schools thanks to the work of a team of researchers at King's College, London during the 1980s. Through academically rigorous trials with learners, the team have helped to cement the approach as one of the most respected and well-researched ways of enhancing learning so far documented.
- The initial focus for the work was in science and was called Cognitive Acceleration Through Science Education (CASE). The project was subsequently developed to encompass other

curriculum areas – maths (CAME), technology (CATE) and geography (CAGE).

- The team leading the work in science devised a series of teaching interventions called 'Thinking Science' which were taught to a group of learners in years 7 and 8 instead of the standard science curriculum.
- The teaching programme challenged children's previous concepts in science and presented them with problems they were unable to solve using current knowledge.
- The CASE programme resulted in significant improvements in learners' science understanding compared to the control group who were taught the standard curriculum, together with greater gains in reasoning ability. Their GCSE results in science were higher than a control group who did not take part in CASE, and also amazingly in maths and English.

Ask yourself

1 To what extent have cognitive acceleration programmes been embraced by your school?

2 What are the key messages of the approach for your classroom?

3 How do cognitive acceleration programmes link with other work taking place in your classroom or school?

✓ To do list

☐ Find out more about the cognitive acceleration programmes currently on offer and what is relevant to your own teaching.

☐ Observe some cognitive acceleration programmes in action in a neighbouring school.

☐ Study in more detail some of the excellent publications available on cognitive acceleration programmes.

Want to find out more?

Adey, P. & Shayer, M. (1994) *Really Raising Standards: Cognitive Intervention and Academic Achievement.* Routledge.

Shayer, M. & Adey, P. (2002) *Learning Intelligence: Cognitive Acceleration Across the Curriculum from 5–15 Years.* Open University Press.

See also . . .

→✣ Evidence-based teaching, page 57.
→✣ Research in education, page 159.

7

Constructivism

What is it?

Constructivism is a set of assumptions governing the way people learn and make sense of the world. It's founded on the premise that, by reflecting on personal experiences, people create their own understanding of the world they live in.

Knowledge bank

- Constructivism is a significant overarching theory that has an important bearing on the day-to-day work of teachers. However, it should be noted that the theory of constructivism was developed to account for *all* types of human learning (i.e. not specifically teacher-mediated learning).
- A principal scholar and point of reference for educationalists interested in constructivism is Swiss philosopher and psychologist Jean Piaget (1896–1980). He suggested that people construct new knowledge by *assimilating* it with their internal

representations of the world. *Accommodation* may be required, by reframing one's view of the world, in order to allow new experiences to fit.

- Constructivism maintains that learning builds on what learners already know. It also includes the concept that learners need to create *personal meaning* from any learning situation – this cannot be 'spoon fed' by a teacher.

- The theory of constructivism also contends that adults can intervene in order to facilitate and promote the learning of children and young people – even though meaning making takes place at the individual level.

- Constructivism also suggests that learning within schools needs to take place in as *contextualized* a way as possible – i.e. that learners need to learn within parameters as close to real life as possible.

- The type of learning taking place in schools can be characterized as *social constructivism*, since it takes place within a collaborative learning environment, orchestrated by a teacher and in the presence of a host of other learners.

- Within constructivism learners are respected as *unique* individuals, with unique backgrounds, culture and needs. Learners are also viewed as complex and multi-dimensional. Furthermore, the responsibility for learning must reside increasingly with the learner, who in turn must be motivated to want to learn. Crucially, learners develop their thinking abilities by interacting with adults – or more able peers.

- Constructivism has given rise to the so-called 'constructivist' approach to teaching, which emphasizes the key role of the learner in personal meaning making in the classroom. It also stresses the need for a 'hands-on' role of learners in the learning process.

- A constructivist learning environment is typified by learners being asked questions rather than the teacher trying to 'transmit' knowledge; learners being asked to explore their understanding rather than being given the right answer; and learners being encouraged to draw their own conclusions, rather than having one imposed. In this sense, teachers move from being instructors to facilitators.

- *Constructionist* approaches, the brain-child of Seymour Papert (1928–), go one step further by suggesting that constructivist approaches are especially effective when people are involved actually *making* something – such as a book, model or computer program. The rapid development of ICT in schools is enabling learners to 'create' in more ways than ever before.
- Some prominent cognitive scientists have cast doubt on the theory of constructivism, contending that the main ideas may be either misleading or that they contradict known findings. Nevertheless, the theory continues to exert a powerful force in schools, adding weight to much modern thinking on effective teaching and learning approaches. It helps to justify what many teachers have traditionally thought as the most effective ways to teach.

Ask yourself

1 To what extent is your classroom underpinned by constructivist principles?
2 What do you see as the benefits of constructivism from an educational point of view? And the drawbacks?
3 What changes does the constructivist approach to teaching suggest might need to be made in your classroom?

✓ To do list

☐ The ideas underpinning constructivism can be difficult to understand, especially for those without a psychology background, yet they have pivotal importance to teachers. Spend an hour doing some internet research on this fascinating topic in order to learn about it.

☐ Create an action plan for embracing more constructivist principles in your classroom.

☐ Work with a like-minded colleague to explore together your views on constructivism and its relevance to your teaching. Ensure you expose yourself to some of the competing theories too.

Want to find out more?

Bransford, J., Brown, A. L. & Cocking, R. R. (2000). *How People Learn: Brain, Mind, Experience, and School*. National Academies Press.

Piaget, J. (1950) *The Psychology of Intelligence*. Routledge.

More information on constructivism is available at
www.learningandteaching.info/learning/constructivism.htm

See also . . .

→❖ Enquiry-based learning, page 50.
→❖ Giving learners a voice, page 65.
→❖ Teaching style, page 175.

8

Continuing professional development

What is it?

Continuing professional development (usually abbreviated to CPD) is the embodiment of lifelong learning for teachers. It represents an expectation that teachers are the lead learners in their schools, and that they embrace and model effective learning themselves.

Knowledge bank

- CPD can take many forms and includes a whole host of different types of activities.
- *Support* from other colleagues provides one of the most effective ways of developing your skills and knowledge. Collaborative approaches to CPD, where teachers prepare lessons together and then reflect on the outcomes, has been highlighted in research as effective.

- Online learning through websites and specialist providers is invaluable. Online services for teachers range from subject-specific sites such as The Association for Science Education (www.ase.org.uk) to general interest sites such as GoogleEarth (www.googleearth.com).
- Teachers' TV has grown in popularity and provides some high-quality examples of genuine success stories in UK schools. Available on pay channel Digital and also on Freeview facilities, Teachers' TV provides useful programmes for viewing or recording for the professional development library.
- *Sabbaticals* outside of the school and also within the school are increasingly common and can take many forms. These could be trips abroad to developing nations on VSO (Voluntary Service Overseas), to specific projects such as funded trips to Australia to look at aspects of ICT in outback teaching. There are places available each year for short-term overseas visits through The Specialist Schools and Academies Trust and via various schemes organized by the British Council. You don't have to be working in a specialist school to apply. Not quite as exotic, but none the less rewarding, one Midlands school offers teachers the opportunity to relinquish management responsibilities to undertake action research for a year, whilst still receiving their full allowance.
- *Performance management*, when carried out in the true spirit of professional development, can provide a rich source of personal and professional growth. In this sense it is characterized by a good deal of ownership over the targets set.
- *In Service Training* (INSET), such as having external facilitators or speakers, is a frequently used tool. It's very important to gain external perspectives in the pressure cooker of a school and a high-quality external INSET provider can energize and fortify colleagues. Always go on recommendations from other schools and take time to plan with an external provider so that you maximize the chances of your needs being met.
- Going outside school for *training courses* can be a most useful opportunity for colleagues to have a high-quality reflective thinking space in the presence of challenging and useful new ideas. Schools who support CPD effectively have structures for enabling colleagues to disseminate learning from external courses upon their return.

- Having a *coach* or *mentor* (→❖ **Coaching,** page 21; **Mentoring,** page 110), for facilitated discussion, collaborative planning or advice has been heralded as a highly effective way of utilizing the intellectual capital of a school. Many schools are setting up collaborative trios or pairings to enable teachers to work in this way.
- Working with *industrial partners* can be a great way of learning about processes outside the school gates.
- *Action research* can provide a focus for developing understanding of processes within your institution and can feed into training days in school led by colleagues.
- *Higher degree* study through attendance or distance learning are further options to explore. Whether you're climbing the career ladder or wish to refresh your perspectives, following a course leading to a higher degree can provide valuable professional learning.

Ask yourself

1 Consider your last three years' CPD experiences. What has been most valuable to you?
2 Consider your professional development goals for the next 12 months – what do you think you need most in terms of support and training?
3 Who do you feel most comfortable working with in your school as you develop professionally? Could you team up with someone in similar circumstances to form a powerful coaching pair?

✓ To do list

☐ Create a professional development portfolio and keep it updated.
☐ Be proactive about your CPD needs and actively research what you need. Budgets are often tight in schools, so consider creative ways to get the support you need, for example through local businesses, tying your needs in closely to overall school improvement targets.
☐ Where you have particular career aspirations, it pays to have a longer term plan, especially where you're considering senior

leadership roles. In this instance you might wish to plan for a higher degree which will require both planning of time and also school budget if you're asking for financial support.

Want to find out more?

Elkin, S. (2006) *CPD Pocketbook*. Teachers' Pocketbooks.

For higher degrees at The Open University visit www.open.ac.uk.

The National Open College Network offers NVQ accredited courses at www.noc.org.uk

TeacherNet is an online resource for teachers set up by the DfES visit at www.teachernet.gov.uk

The Specialist Schools and Academies Trust is at www.specialistschools.org.uk/tipd

See also . . .

Any of the other briefings have clear links to CPD.

9

Creativity across the curriculum

What is it?

Creativity is the process of finding and implementing new and appropriate ways of thinking and doing. People who are able to do so with ease are often said to be '*creative*', but there are dangers of pigeon-holing people in this way (see below).

Knowledge bank

- Though traditionally thought of as referring to the 'creative arts' (music, art, theatre), creativity has relevance to *all* subject areas.
- Creativity across the curriculum is a much neglected area of schools' practice which is only just beginning to receive the attention it deserves.
- Creativity can be defined in various ways, including the definition above as well as 'the purposeful search for innovation in problem solving' (Best and Thomas 2007).

- Creativity is a *process* with a number of clearly identifiable stages (see diagram) – the skills to be creative can be taught and learnt.

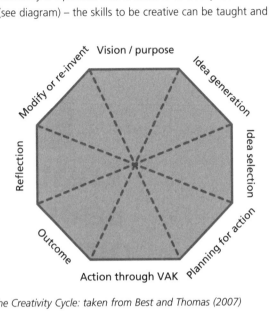

The Creativity Cycle: taken from Best and Thomas (2007)

- Teachers need to be creative to new ways of teaching and learners need to be creative in order to live successful and happy lives. We believe that creativity is a vital human attribute that will enable people to flourish in the uncertain world of tomorrow.
- Creativity also allows teachers and school leaders to adapt to changing circumstances, allowing them to keep their practice at the cutting edge.
- Teaching creative skills can be infused into lessons within one subject area or taught discretely – a blended approach combining the two is likely to get the best results.
- Because creativity is about opening up to new possibilities it's essential that you adopt an open-critical approach if you are to continue to develop your own creativity. This includes opening up to what your learners have to say about effective teaching and learning.

Ask yourself

1 To what extent do you recognize the importance of creativity to the subjects you teach?

2 In what ways do you currently use creative approaches in your teaching? How could these be developed in the future?

3 How do you currently try to help your learners develop their creative skills? What could you do to allow them to develop these skills more?

✓ To do list

☐ Carry out a 'creativity audit' over the course of a week, identifying creative practice in your own and another teacher's classroom.

☐ Reflect on the kinds of creative skills that you would like learners to develop in the subject(s) you teach – draw up an action plan outlining how you can ensure that these skills are developed more systematically by more learners over the next half-term.

☐ Visit a neighbouring school with the express mission of finding an effective teaching and learning approach that has not been tried in your school. Take it back to your school and try to work with other colleagues to embed practice in your school too.

Want to find out more?

Best, B. & Thomas, W. (2007) *The Creative Teaching and Learning Toolkit.* Continuum International Publishing.

Best, B. & Thomas, W. (to be published 2008) *The Creative Teaching and Learning Resource Book.* Continuum International Publishing.

Sternberg, R. ed. (1999) *The Handbook of Creativity.* Cambridge University Press.

The authors run courses on Creativity across the curriculum – details from www.creativity4learning.co.uk

See also . . .

→❖ Accelerated learning, page 5.

→❖ Active learning, page 9.

→❖ Constructivism, page 27.

→❖ Evidence-based teaching, page 57.

10

Differentiation

What is it?

Differentiation is the process of tailoring learning experiences to the needs of individual learners. The aim is that each learner can be enabled to reach his or her potential.

Knowledge bank

- The essence of differentiation is that effective teaching is about working with *individual learners*, not classes or groups.
- The challenge for teachers is to design learning experiences that are accessible and engaging for all the learners in a class.
- There are obvious links between differentiation and →❖ **Personalization in education** (page 146), as both seek to ensure that the needs of individuals are catered for.
- While this does not mean that you need to create an individual learning plan for every learner in every lesson, it does mean that you need to reflect on the *learning differences* and →❖ **Learning**

preferences (page 86) of your learners before you can design effective learning experiences.

- The factors that need to be borne in mind before differentiation can take place include the individual's:
  - ability level in the subject or task
  - barriers to learning: psychological, physical or social
  - learning style preferences: the mix of auditory, visual, kinaesthetic for example
  - motivation level
  - social and cultural background
  - physical size, shape and structure of the learner.
- As such, differentiation can be seen to encompass a wider spectrum than simply the ability of learners, which has traditionally been seen as the key focus of differentiation.
- Various strategies can be used by teachers to differentiate learning experiences, including varying:
  - the depth of learning
  - the breadth of learning
  - the tasks set
  - the difficulty of stimulus materials
  - the resources themselves to make them more accessible
  - the support given to learners
  - the degree of independent learning.
- These strategies can be used with varying *frequency* as well as with varying degrees of *magnitude*, so that learners experience the differentiation strategies only some of the time and to varying extents.
- Although in general it's not helpful to pigeon-hole learners, it is possible to distinguish several types of learners for whom differentiation is especially significant:
  - very able learners
  - very weak learners
  - learners with a special educational need
  - learners with dual exceptionality (e.g. very able *and* with a special educational need).
- The diagram overleaf illustrates how the magnitude and frequency of use of the various differentiation techniques can vary with different types of learners.

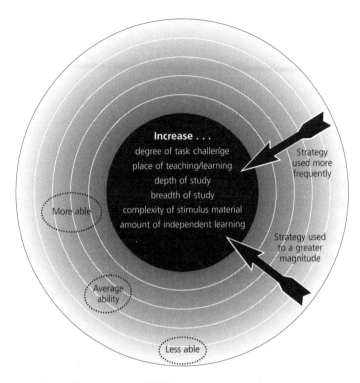

Adapted from Best et al. (2006)

Ask yourself

1 What differentiation strategies do you currently use?
2 Are there any individual learning differences or preferences that you do not currently cater for to the extent you would like?
3 What specific strategies could you use to address these?
4 Consider one of your more challenging classes – which learners most need differentiation and what strategies need to be used to ensure these learners can access the curriculum?

✓ To do list

☐ Review the differentiation strategies you use in the light of the information in this briefing.

☐ Consider implementing new strategies to target particular learners.

☐ Study the diagram and consider the strengths and weaknesses of the different differentiation techniques.

Want to find out more?

O'Brien, T. & Guiney, D. (2001) *Differentiation in Teaching and Learning: Principles and Practice.* Continuum International Publishing.

Dodge, J. (2006) *Differentiation in Action: A Complete Resource with Research-supported Strategies to Help You Plan and Organize Differentiated Instruction.* Teaching strategies.

Stradling, R., Saunders, L. & Weston, P. (1991) *Differentiation in Action: Whole School Approach for Raising Attainment.* The Stationery Office Books.

See also . . .

→✣ More able learners, page 122.

→✣ Personalization in education, page 146.

→✣ Streaming, setting, banding or mixed-ability teaching?, page 168.

Drama across the curriculum

What is it?

Drama involves the use of the voice and/or body to act out a character or to simulate an object, in order to express a viewpoint, emotion or to put across information. It has always had a place in teaching and for some teachers forms a key component of the classroom climate they create.

Knowledge bank

- Drama has the potential to invigorate the teaching of any subject area, allowing learners to gain new insights into the subject matter or concepts they're investigating in a highly engaging way.
- In purely curricular terms, at present drama doesn't appear as a subject in its own right within the English/Welsh National Curriculum and curriculum guidance has generally ignored the contribution that drama makes.

- Drama appears simply as a statutory requirement as part of the 'speaking and listening' strand of the National Curriculum for English. This requires that learners participate in a variety of drama activities to ensure that they:
  - use language and actions to explore and convey situations, characters and emotions
  - create and sustain roles when working individually and with others
  - comment constructively on drama they have watched or in which they have taken part.
- The Scottish 5–14 guidelines, however, do recognize the value of drama and make specific reference to it, stating that it should provide all learners with opportunities to:
  - reach new understandings and appreciation of self, others and the environment through imaginative dramatic experience
  - communicate ideas and feelings through language, expression and movement, in real and imaginary contexts
  - develop confidence and self-esteem in their day-to-day interaction with others
  - develop sensitivity towards the feelings, opinions and values of others through purposeful interaction
  - develop a range of dramatic skills and techniques.
- Drama offers a number of key *benefits* to learners and can be applied across the wider curriculum, regardless of the age of the learners:
  - *Accessibility*: For the majority of learners drama is the most easily accessible form of art. It does not require mastery of a musical instrument or a specific level of competency in painting or reading in order for learners to be able to express themselves. It is a natural development of the communication skills which they're acquiring elsewhere through play. Their familiarity with the media of film and television means that learners are used to relating to expressing ideas in this manner. It is essentially an extension and refinement of these areas rooted in life and human interaction. Use of movement, language, gesture and facial expression in order to convey meaning are concepts with which learners are already familiar, even if they have not yet reached the point of verbalizing them as such.

- *Drama as group activity*: Learning via drama is a sharing experience, similar to play, in which imagined worlds can be explored. It is an active experience which requires collaboration between parties.
- *Drama as process*: In this genre there is no external audience for the work, but there is an essential internal audience which leads to evaluation and discussion.

• Process is more important than the 'product' in drama and this is seen as a creative exercise, where the creativity is the application of the imagination to problem-solving activities. The activity is generated in response to a stimulus (e.g. textual stimulus such as a newspaper article, visual stimulus such as a cartoon, aural stimulus such as music or a specific sound such as an air-raid warning siren or an artefact/prop).

Ask yourself

1 To what extent do you already use drama in your classroom?
2 How do you use it? How do your learners use it?
3 To what extent can you envisage drama being a useful tool within your subject area?
4 What barriers exist to your own use at present? What barriers exist to your learners' use? How might they be overcome?

✓ To do list

☐ Try to incorporate a new drama activity into one of your lessons over the next month.
☐ Ask your learners what their opinions are of using drama in lessons.
☐ Observe a colleague who is passionate about the use of drama in his or her subject.

Want to find out more?

Radcliffe, B. (2007) *The Drama for Learning Pocketbook*. Teachers' Pocketbooks.

Rooyackers, P. (1997) *101 Drama Games for Children: Fun and Learning with Acting and Make-believe.* Hunter House Smartfun Book.

See also ...

→✣ Accelerated learning, page 5.
→✣ Active learning, page 9.
→✣ Personalization in education, page 146.

Emotional intelligence

What is it?

Emotional intelligence (sometimes known as *emotional literacy* and quantified as EQ as opposed to IQ) is a form of intelligence that involves the ability to have an appropriate relationship with our own emotions and those of other people, to discriminate between them and then to use the information to guide our thoughts and deeds.

Knowledge bank

- The research of US researchers Salovey and Mayer brought the term emotional intelligence into our thinking in the early 1990s. Daniel Goleman's groundbreaking book *Emotional Intelligence: Why It Can Matter More Than IQ* was published in 1995 and this further brought the concept into the mainstream.
- Howard Gardner's work on →✣ **Multiple intelligences** (page 129) similarly fed into the discussions about emotional

intelligence in the 1990s, as it relates to Gardner's inter- and intra-personal intelligences. These are the ability to relate to others and to ourselves respectively.

- Most writers on emotional intelligence seem to categorize the features of emotionally intelligent function in the following or similar categories:
  - *Self-awareness* Having objectivity about our own feelings and noticing them as they occur. This self-awareness is characterized by confidence, a sense of integrity, self-honesty, openness and appropriate levels of self-esteem.
  - *Emotional management* Constructively managing our feelings and recognizing the useful information that lies behind them is key. In particular, having due awareness of the values and beliefs that lie beneath emotional responses and the impact of experiences in both aligning with those values and beliefs and misaligning. Through this thoughtfulness we can develop constructive ways to handle our emotional responses. This does not mean suppressing emotions, but it does mean respecting them and being aware of the information they bring.
  - *Being a self-starter* This involves using emotions positively to reach the individual and team goals we wish for. We need to be emotionally aware enough to ensure that goals are motivating and yet balance our own needs with the needs of others. This enables us to delay short-term gain, to make progress towards our longer-term goals.
  - *Empathic relationships* Being sensitive towards the needs and feelings of others and understanding that people are different and have different needs. This includes being aware of, and handling other people's emotions competently and without allowing our own emotions to impact on this negatively. It also encompasses respecting and upholding the values and beliefs of ourselves and others in our interactions.
- Developing emotional intelligence comes from the practice of encouraging reflection on our emotions and our actions. In classrooms this comes through seeking opportunities to use events within the classroom and also happenings in the wider world and asking reflective questions of learners.

- Cath Corrie in her book *Becoming Emotionally Intelligent*, talks of Emotional Wisdom. She defines this as 'the ability to use our emotional intelligence to contribute to our families, our communities and to humanity as a whole'. She goes on to suggest that one of the most effective ways that children can learn emotional intelligence and develop emotional wisdom is to have it modelled by their teachers.
- The practice of coaching has been described as 'emotional intelligence in action' and provides a set of principles and practice for teachers to become even more emotionally intelligent in their classroom responses (→✦ **Coaching**, page 21).

Ask yourself

1 What currently are your strengths in developing emotional intelligence in your classroom? What do you need to work on?
2 How are you modelling good emotionally intelligent practice at school?
3 What opportunities are there for encouraging further reflection on emotional issues in your classroom?

✔ To do list

☐ Study one of the excellent texts on emotional intelligence.
☐ Reflect on your own emotional intelligence and consider what habits you would like to develop in this area.
☐ Seek an EQ buddy in a colleague or friend to help you both to reflect on emotional aspects of your work. It's particularly important to have an objective partner where your emotions are involved. Set up mutually agreeable ground rules for working together in this area, such as:
  − stick to reporting what you observe, rather than what you think it means
  − what is discussed between us, stays between us
  − it's never personal . . . and so on.
Encourage this kind of buddying between learners, too.

Want to find out more?

Corrie, C. (2003) *Becoming Emotionally Intelligent*. Network Educational Press.

Goleman, D. (1995) *Emotional Intelligence: Why It Can Matter More Than IQ*. Bloomsbury.

Capacchione, L. (2001) *Living with Feeling*. Rider Books.

Zabat-Zinn, J. (1996) *Full Catastrophe Living*. Piatkus.

See also . . .

→❖ Accelerated learning, page 5.

→❖ Coaching, page 21.

→❖ Learning preferences, page 86.

→❖ Multiple intelligences, page 129.

→❖ Personalization in education, page 146.

Enquiry-based learning

What is it?

Enquiry-based learning is a method of learning that allows learners to progress through a series of logical steps in response to a question. It is often used for independent learning projects over a lengthy period of time.

Knowledge bank

- Enquiry-based learning originally developed in science, but is now used widely in other subjects, especially geography and history.
- The approach requires learners to work through a set learning sequence in response to a stimulus question, typically:
  - introduction
  - data collection
  - data presentation
  - data analysis
  - conclusion
  - evaluation.

- The approach also provides the structure for a written report which is usually produced to complete the enquiry.
- The approach is highly suitable for giving to learners as an independent learning project which can be worked on for a number of lessons. For example, learners carrying out GCSE coursework in a range of subjects now typically follow the enquiry route.
- Once learners are engaged in an enquiry it is not unusual for the teacher to keep quiet for much of the lesson, letting learners work at their own pace through tasks and providing individual guidance as required.
- Enquiry-based learning allows learners to ask deep questions about the subject matter and carry out their own real-life experiments, gathering data and producing their own reports. As such it can be a very engaging and stimulating learning method and has sometimes been called 'real-world learning'.
- The approach provides learners with valuable transferable skills in problem-solving and report writing, which can be used in later life.
- The approach places great emphasis on learners taking ownership of their own learning and fits well with the current drive to put learners at the heart of the learning process.

Ask yourself

1 What examples of enquiry-based learning are there currently in your school? And in specific subjects?
2 What benefits could enquiry-based learning bring to the subjects you teach?
3 How might an active method of learning such as this help to engage learners in the subject(s) you teach? What might the challenges be?

✓ To do list

☐ If you're not familiar with the approach, observe a colleague teaching using enquiry-based learning.

☐ Consider the practicalities of how enquiry-based learning can be applied to your subject area.

☐ Experiment with using the approach in your classroom, explaining first to learners what it is and how you plan to use it. Then gather feedback from a wide range of sources on how effective it is in your classroom.

☐ If you and your learners become experienced at enquiry-based learning, consider asking learners to set the questions themselves.

Want to find out more?

Haynes, J. (2001) *Children as Philosophers: Learning Through Enquiry and Dialogue in the Primary Classroom.* Routledge Falmer.

Roberts, M. (2003) *Learning Through Enquiry: Making Sense of the Key Stage 3 Classroom.* Geographical Association.

See also . . .

→❖ Accelerated learning, page 5.

→❖ Active learning, page 9.

→❖ Constructivism, page 27.

14

Every child matters

What is it?

Every Child Matters, subtitled 'Change for Children', is a UK government approach to the development of multi-level, multi-agency support for children and young people, in the interests of ensuring their safety, health and well-being from birth, up to the age of 19.

Knowledge bank

- Every Child Matters (ECM) came about as a result of a government review of support for children following the Victoria Climbié case and inquiry. It is the government's aim for every child, whatever their background or their circumstances, to have the support they need to:
  - be healthy
  - stay safe
  - enjoy and achieve

- make a positive contribution
- achieve economic well-being.

- These five strands form the basis of the 'Outcomes Framework' for support. For each of the aims laid out there are a series of target indicators and inspection criteria – see below.
- There is a Common Assessment Framework (CAF) which consists of a three-part process for assessing the needs of children and young people: Preparation, Discussion and Delivery.
- There is a strong emphasis in ECM on multi-agency cooperation between schools, social services, justice, voluntary and health services. *Children's Trusts* exist to bring together these groups of services in local areas. These trusts, whilst not being legal entities, are partnerships with common outcomes for children set out by the ECM framework. ECM is, however, underpinned by the

Every child matters

Be happy	Stay safe	Enjoy and achieve	Make a positive contribution	Achieve economic well-being
AIMS	AIMS	AIMS	AIMS	AIMS
Be physically healthy	Be safe from maltreatment, neglect, violence and sexual exploitation	Be ready for school	Engage in decision-making and support the community and environment	Engage in further education, employment or training on leaving school
Be mentally and emotionally healthy		Attend and enjoy school		
Be sexually healthy	Be safe from accidents and injury	Achieve stretching national educational standards at primary school	Engage in law-abiding and positive behaviour in and out of school	Be ready for employment
Have healthy lifestyles	Be safe from bullying and discrimination			Live in decent homes and sustainable communities
Choose not to take illegal drugs		Achieve personal and social development and enjoy recreation	Develop positive relationships and choose not to bully or discriminate	
	Be safe from anti-social behaviour in and out of school			Have access to transport and material goods
	Have security, stability and are cared for	Achieve stretching national educational standards at secondary school	Develop self-confidence and successfully deal with significant life changes and challenges	Live in households free from low income
			Develop enterprising behaviour	

Children Act 2004 and this sets out the duty of those involved in children's and young people's services to cooperate and to focus on improving outcomes for all children and young people.

- The Children's Trusts exist so that the organizations involved with providing services to children will team up in more regulated ways to share information and protect children and young people to achieve their ambitions and stay out of harm's way. The aim of the trusts is for professionals and volunteers to work in effective multi-disciplinary teams, have joint training and develop common approaches to working together.

- The trusts involve children and young people in the process of providing support and inspection processes, and in part, inspectors draw on the views of local children and young people.

- The trusts are supported by integrated processes across all services. Some processes, like the CAF, will be centrally driven, others will be devised locally. At local level it is likely that common approaches will add detail through:
  - A joint assessment of needs
  - Making decisions together within Children's Trusts
  - Being aware of available resources and utilizing them
  - Planning together to deploy resources

- Whilst schools are integral to this approach they are likely to play a significant role in their own right as the interface with children and young people on a daily basis. ECM expects that all schools actively seek to engage parents in children and young people's education, helping parents to support what they can do at home to help their child's education.

Ask yourself

1 What aspects of the ECM agenda are you able to influence?
2 Which areas of the ECM framework are you supporting most effectively?
3 Consider individual children or young people with whom you work that cause you concern. How does this framework clarify your thinking about the actions you need to take to support them?

✓ To do list

☐ Using the Outcomes Framework as an audit tool, consider each area and rate your support against each strand where 1 is not at all supporting and 5 consistently supporting.

☐ From the audit, consider the areas you would need to address. Decide what support you might need to progress these areas and seek it.

☐ Discuss the ECM agenda with colleagues and identify the extent to which they are aware of their duties to it.

Want to find out more?

More information can be found at www.everychildmatters.gov.uk

See also . . .

→✣ National strategies for schools, page 133.
→✣ Personalization in education, page 146.

15

Evidence-based teaching

What is it?

Evidence-based teaching is teaching that benefits from research into what works best in the classroom. It takes its point of reference from research conducted principally in the field of education psychology.

Knowledge bank

- Much of what we do in the classroom is influenced by our own experience – evidence-based teaching takes this one step further by using the experience of thousands of teachers, and of expert researchers into teaching and learning, to design the most effective learning experiences.
- The body of evidence that supports this approach is located principally within research journals into education – especially so-called 'meta studies' that draw together findings from many (sometimes hundreds) of previous studies.

- An important principle embodied by evidence-based teaching is that while there are many *potential* teaching and learning approaches that have been shown to get positive results, teachers need to be able to distinguish those that have the *maximum* benefit.
- Evidence-based teaching seeks to place education on the same footing as medicine and other fields of endeavour that are informed by *objective* evidence of what does and does not work. While acknowledging the complexity of education compared to other more 'scientific' research disciplines, advocates of evidence-based teaching maintain that there is much we *do* know that can be used by teachers to design more effective learning experiences.
- Evidence-based research principally uses findings from the field of education psychology – the closest we have to the 'science' underpinning effective teaching. Rigorous studies based in schools are, however, surprisingly rare and we often rely on more carefully controlled research carried out in other settings.
- The education consultant Geoff Petty has done most to put evidence-based teaching on the map in the UK, thanks to his influential writings on the subject.
- There are clear links between evidence-based teaching and the concept of ⇢❖ **Research in education** (page 159) generally.

Ask yourself

1 To what extent is your current teaching based on research evidence?
2 What are the main sources of evidence you use as a teacher to make judgements about the techniques you use? How reliable are these?
3 What are the main challenges confronting a teacher wishing to use evidence-based approaches in their classroom?

✓ To do list

☐ Make time to scan an education research journal once a term in order to learn more about the latest approaches. If you're finding it difficult to track down a suitable publication, encourage your school's CPD coordinator to subscribe to the *British Educational Research Journal* for your staff library.

☐ Consider engaging with some action research in your own school – partnerships can often be made with higher education institutions, or you could form a research group with like-minded colleagues.

☐ Education research conferences are great ways to learn about new and exciting approaches, as well as allowing you to mix with researchers and the world of education psychology. Find out about one in easy reach of your school and get involved.

Want to find out more?

Petty, G. (2006) *Evidence-based Teaching.* Nelson Thornes.

See also . . .

→❖ Cognitive acceleration programmes, page 24.
→❖ Research in education, page 159.
→❖ Self-evaluation, page 162.

16

Gender awareness

What is it?

Gender awareness is to do with understanding how the gender of a learner can impact on the teaching and learning situation and adopting strategies that take this into account in order to allow each learner to reach his/her full potential.

Knowledge bank

- There's an ongoing debate as to whether single sex teaching actually improves boys' and girls' attainment, and boys' attainment in particular (→❖ **Streaming, setting, banding or mixed ability teaching?**, page 168).
- Historically, there have always been single sex schools in this country and although the majority of schools are now co-educational (mixed sex) there are still several which are not. A number of mixed sex schools also adopt the strategy of teaching certain subjects in single sex classes.

- DfES research (*Single Sex Teaching in a Co-educational Comprehensive School*) during the 1990s indicated that those taught in this way achieved better results than boys and girls nationally – with proportionally better results for the boys. However, there is still little evidence on the long-term effectiveness of this strategy.
- Studies in this area have shown that although the classes were a positive and successful experience for both sexes, they did require considerable commitment from staff and should not be simply seen as a knee-jerk reaction to addressing the issue of potential underachievement by boys.
- An important step is to always be aware of your own prejudices – to be able to address a stereotype you first have to be able to recognize it. Self-awareness is essential if you are to teach in a way that encourages others to be confident in relation to these issues.
- There still exists a number of stereotypes as regards the role of men and women in society and while successive generations may challenge these, it's important to recognize that parental cooperation is important in this area. By encouraging learners to challenge stereotypes and broaden their own horizons we can help to break down some of the barriers to equality. However, it's essential that this is not done by disparaging some of the traditional roles – equality should be about giving a broad choice, not about negating choice.
- For example, it's important that a girl who wants to work with children does not feel that her choice is regarded as 'second class' in comparison to a girl who wants to work with computers, any more than a male nurse is made to feel second rate in comparison to a male doctor. In each case the individual is making a choice based upon their own talents – and each choice is equally valid.
- Try not to think of gender in simplistic terms and always to remember that there are huge differences *amongst* women and *amongst* men. There is always a danger in working with assumptions. For example, in relation to ICT there's sometimes a tendency to assume that women are more interested in the functional and communicative use of ICT while men are more interested in playing with the computer and understanding how it works. It is, therefore, important to offer a wide range of

activities which allow both sexes to explore the full potential of ICT in order to break away from this kind of assumption.

- It's also important that the activities are presented in such a way that there is not seen to be any specific gender expectation. The same holds true for other curriculum subjects – for example within drama there's scope for both male and female learners to be equally involved in costume, set and lighting design.

- When thinking about gender issues it's all too easy to lose sight of one of the most basic tenets of education: that each learner is an individual and therefore has particular learning preferences. In thinking about how best to teach 'boys' or how to motivate 'girls' do not forget that we are trying to teach *individual* learners.

- Positive role models are essential. Within education at present the profession is suffering a gender imbalance. There are more female secondary teachers than males, but less in leadership roles; the vast majority of design technology teachers are men and food technology teachers women; in primary schools eight out of ten headteachers are female. As a result, rather than dispelling gender stereotypes many schools are actually reinforcing them and will continue to do so until more men are attracted into teaching and men and women have equal access to different subjects and senior positions.

- An effective school equality policy must be something which is 'live', not just a paper document. Too many schools still refer to 'dinner ladies' and 'cleaning ladies', even when there are male team members. Staff of both sexes should be seen to be active in all areas of school life. What goes on outside the classroom is as important as what goes on inside it – the messages must reinforce one another so that the whole school ethos reflects what's happening in the classroom.

- Language awareness is crucial – even in informal staffroom situations. It is still not uncommon to find staff talking differently to and about female learners.

- Having said the above males and females at secondary school do in general behave differently and it's important that schools are aware of these gender issues when formulating policies on behaviour management. Indeed, it appears that the brains of males and females are 'wired' in different ways – so it's important to recognize this when dealing with gender issues.

- The DfES study, *Making the Grade but Feeling Distressed,* concluded that although girls often perform better than boys, they are generally more vulnerable to mental distress.
- DfES research has tended to support the idea that girls are more motivated to study modern foreign languages in general than boys, and more inclined to identify with speakers of a foreign language. Their study showed that in class they tried harder and believed more in the value of making an effort. In terms of preference between languages, boys tended to be more motivated to study German than French. German was felt to be more 'masculine' than French, but boys tended not to try hard at any language because the work is described as 'tedious'.
- DfES research on the relationship between gender and science indicated that both boys' and girls' attitudes to science vary over time, related to the quality of the curriculum, the quality of the teacher, and perceived career benefits, with boys predominant at A-level physics. However, it was found that a 'gender-inclusive' approach to teaching science, which incorporated values and extends both boys' and girls' prior experiences and learning, was popular with both sexes.
- Within English lessons girls appear to thrive in secondary classrooms as they currently outperform boys in English SATs and in almost all GCSE subjects. However, although girls seemingly outstrip boys at Key Stages 3 and 4, it has been observed that classroom talk does not always in fact reflect the state of female achievement suggested by exam results. Male learners tend to dominate classroom talk, with teachers focusing more often on encouraging male participation. By excluding girls from classroom talk, the girls are being denied the opportunities necessary to develop higher-level cognitive skills.

Ask yourself

1 To what extent are you aware of gender issues on a day-to-day basis?
2 How do you work to encourage positive equality of opportunity in your classroom?
3 How do your learners perceive gender issues within the subject(s) you teach?

4 What barriers exist to your own promotion of gender equality and how may these be overcome?

5 How can you promote a more positive view of gender issues in your classroom?

✓ To do list

☐ Look over an illustrated book that is used commonly in your classroom. Identify in what ways genders are stereotyped and the implications for your learners.

☐ Consider your own use of language and that of your learners when discussing gender issues. Now consider your own use of language and that of your learners when referring to one another in informal situations – identify the differences between the two situations and consider what the implications of this are for your work.

☐ Prepare an action plan designed to help yourself and your learners become more sensitive to gender issues in the year ahead.

Want to find out more?

The Equal Opportunities Commission (www.eoc.org.uk) has produced a range of useful documents, including: Gaps, Traps and Stereotypes: educating for sex equality *and* Equal Opportunities Guide for Parents.

The Department for Trade and Industry (www.dti.gov.uk) has produced an equality teaching resource pack entitled *Does Sex Make a Difference?*
www.rcss.ed.ac.uk/sigis/public/theme/schooleducation
www.standards.dfes.gov.uk/research/themes/gender

See also . . .

→❖ Inclusion, page 78.
→❖ Learning preferences, page 86.
→❖ Streaming, setting, banding or mixed-ability teaching?, page 168.
→❖ Underachievement, page 192.

17

Giving learners a voice

What is it?

Giving learners a voice refers to the process where the views of children and young people are used to improve the educational offering of schools. It involves actively *listening* to what learners have to say and then, within reason, *acting* on the suggestions they have made. A series of recent studies has shown that it is a much under-used tool for school improvement, despite being capable of getting powerful results.

Knowledge bank

- The philosophy for respecting the voice of learners in schools is rooted in the belief that, as the beneficiaries of the education services of schools, children and young people should have a lot to say about how they can be improved.
- For schools to genuinely open up to the power of giving learners a voice, there is a need for them to accept that adults do not

always have the *right* answers. There is also a requirement for teachers, school leaders and other school staff to embrace the views of young people in a positive way. This can be hard for some people to do – especially those with a traditional view of education.

- The move to personalize education (→✧ **Personalization in education**, page 146) and a range of recent government measures have encouraged schools to open up to the views of learners in a way that was not possible before. Schools are being increasingly encouraged to enter into a dialogue with learners about how schools are run and lessons taught. Some teachers have found this transition difficult, perhaps due to concerns that their professionalism is in some way questioned by respecting the voice of learners.

- In parallel with the above, children and young people are playing increasingly important roles in schools. This includes work at the classroom level, where they are giving feedback to teachers on lessons or even observing learning episodes as 'expert learners'. It also involves more strategic issues, such as representing the views of other youngsters on the School Council or even taking part in interviews for new staff.

- Studies have repeatedly shown that, when invited to give their opinions on a whole raft of school issues, learners – even very young children – can make insightful and helpful observations and suggestions. Indeed, it is extremely rare to find examples of learners using such opportunities to 'get at' individual teachers or make other inappropriate remarks.

- Respecting the voice of learners *does not* mean that you simply adopt every new measure that is proposed by them – this misconception has undermined the engagement of many teachers who fear a 'free for all'. Instead, the situation can be likened to a staff meeting or parental consultation session – you listen to the views of others, and provide a forum for them to be aired, but then make decisions based on your own professional judgement and years of experience. However, those teachers and school leaders who have benefited most from this type of work have recognized that their own opinions need to be challenged – and importantly – sometimes changed.

- There are some very advanced models for using the learner voice to improve education, which if you're prepared to take the bold step, could really transform your classroom. To embrace these you'll need to adopt a radically different view about the power relationships in your classroom and begin to accept that the real power rests with the learners, not you as a teacher.

Ask yourself

1 To what extent do you *genuinely* listen to what learners have to say and *act* upon their suggestions.

2 How often do you open up dialogue in your classroom to enable learners to have their say and influence the direction of learning?

3 Are you still sceptical about the value of using learners' views to improve their education? If so what is holding you back? If not how can you help other people in your school to take a more enlightened approach?

✓ To do list

☐ Identify as many ways as you can that illustrate how you have used the voice of learners to enhance what happens in your classroom.

☐ If this is something you feel passionate about, talk with senior managers about how you can develop a better school-wide climate for using the voice of learners as a tool for school improvement.

☐ Do some focused reading on the topic of the learner voice, as there are some very radical models that are sure to take things to another level in your school.

Want to find out more?

The classic text on this subject is a must read for those committed to school improvement:

Flutter, J. & Ruddock, J. (2003) *How to Improve Your School: Giving Pupils a Voice.* Continuum International Publishing.

See also . . .

→❖ Constructivism, page 27.

→❖ Enquiry-based learning, page 50.

→❖ Teaching style, page 175.

18

Hypnosis in education

What is it?

Hypnosis is the phenomenon of deep relaxation which has vital but currently under-tapped potential as a tool for more effective teaching and learning. The subject is, however, somewhat unfairly shrouded in controversy.

Knowledge bank

- Hypnosis has many taboos and much folklore associated with it, and this is in part due to the use of deep trance hypnosis for stage shows and its misrepresentation in fiction writing as a tool for gaining power over others. In fact, it provides a very positive state of mind whereby problems can be resolved and learning can take place with ease. All hypnosis is in fact self-induced as a person must be willing to go into this relaxed state.
- Historically hypnosis has been practised for thousands of years in healing rituals in India and ancient Egypt. In subsequent centuries

it has been used by some doctors to treat a wide range of conditions, but has remained on the fringes of medical practice. The big names in hypnosis such as Erickson, Estabrooks and Elts and their followers have continued to use the process to support mental, emotional and physical healing, with great success. Light trance states can have potentially useful spin-offs for learners in helping create relaxed alertness, improving memory and in building self-esteem.

- There is little doubt that hypnosis in an educational setting *could* be seen as controversial. Yet teachers might be surprised to find that trance is a state of mind which is naturally occurring in their learners (and themselves) every day. When a learner stares unmoving into space for a few moments they have entered a light state of trance. When we drive to work and don't remember consciously how we made it through certain parts of the journey because we were 'in a world of our own', we were in trance.

- There is a school of thought that says that anything that presupposes trance, causes trance, so it is possible that just sitting here reading this book, feeling the seat beneath you, and reading down . . . the page . . . is allowing you to go into a light state of trance. Indeed, reading itself takes us into light states of trance too.

- In classrooms, trance can be useful to help learners put aside their concerns and fears about the 'risks' of learning and focus on learning more fully. It can also be useful to enable children to be more receptive to positive affirmations about their work and about themselves. In this sense it can support self-esteem building processes.

- Natural and simple ways to help learners relax into light trance (i.e. where learners are in a relaxed state of alertness) are through telling stories, and through providing them with guided visualizations, or through providing quiet reflection time to consider an issue or challenge. Finger tapping (where the thumb on each hand is sequentially touched by each finger from forefinger, to middle finger to ring to little and back) occupies the conscious mind and can be a useful process in releasing creative thoughts in problem-solving, as can counting backwards from 100 out loud, whilst a learner draws a solution to the challenge on paper.

- Isn't hypnosis dangerous? The kinds of light states of relaxation created by stories and visualizations are perfectly safe if the language used is positive and resourceful. All trance is self-induced, a person who does not want to relax into trance will not do so. You would need specialist training to facilitate deeper levels of trance and this would be inappropriate in a classroom setting anyway.

Ask yourself

1 When are your naturally occurring trance times in the day?
2 How often do you use stories, metaphors and visualizations in your teaching? Consider the positive messages and subject content you can pass across built into the stories and visualizations.
3 What experiences do you have of your subconscious mind offering solutions, ideas and questions?

✓ To do list

☐ Find out more about hypnosis through reading or attending courses.
☐ Consider ways in which you are already providing periods of relaxed reflection for learners. Think about ways in which you can offer positive suggestions to them about their ability to solve their own problems and be resourceful.
☐ Talk to colleagues about ways in which they support learning through enabling children to block out the self-conscious part of their mind (the conscious part).

Want to find out more?

James, T., Flores, L. & Schober, J. (2000) *Hypnosis: A Comprehensive Guide.* Crown House Publishing.
For information on constructing light trance-inducing stories see:
Best, B. & Thomas, W. (2007) *The Creative Teaching and Learning Toolkit.* Continuum International Publishing.

Attend a course on trance work: Vision for Learning Ltd run courses in NLP, and Hypnosis for Teachers: www.visionforlearning.co.uk/learning.htm

See also . . .

→❖ Creativity across the curriculum, page 35.
→❖ Neuro-linguistic programming, page 136.
→❖ Metaphor, page 113.

19

ICT across the curriculum

What is it?

Information and Communications Technology Across the Curriculum (*ICTAC*), is a government initiative to embed the use of ICT into all subject areas. It forms part of the ICT strand of the Key Stage 3 National Strategy. The aim is that learners and teachers will use ICT effectively in every subject area, as an essential tool to enhance teaching and learning. ICT across the curriculum can also be recognized as an aspect of teachers' work which is not linked to any specific government initiative and is instead about ensuring that the appropriate technology and tools are used to promote effective learning.

Knowledge bank

- As part of their responsibilities for ICT in the National Curriculum, schools are required to ensure that learners are given opportunities to apply and develop ICT capability across the curriculum.

- The government's recent drive to enhance the role of ICT within subject areas is a welcome opportunity for teachers to think again about how they use this important teaching and learning tool – however, it can also been seen as a logical extension of what teachers have been doing to enhance learning through ICT.
- Embedding ICT in subject teaching is seen as a government priority for extending learning opportunities for all learners, now that a 'critical mass' of technology and connectivity is in place.
- The argument has moved on from *whether* ICT can aid learning to *how* teachers can take advantage of it in specific subject areas.
- A key principle is to move ICT from a discrete subject which is taught separately to the main curriculum, to one which is fully integrated into subject areas.
- The government's vision, which is surely shared by most teachers, is that ICT can be integrated seamlessly into every subject area.
- Every school should have a designated 'ICTAC coordinator' who is responsible for overseeing the use of ICT across the curriculum – this is sometimes, but not always, the ICT coordinator and is often a senior manager.
- Schools are able to choose ICTAC as one of their areas of focus as part of the wider Key Stage 3 Strategy initiatives, and will then be supported by a local lead consultant for ICTAC in the local authority.
- The DfES framework for ICT capability identifies 10 key concepts which describe the breadth of ICT capability and progression in learning through Key Stage 3. These provide a useful vehicle when considering how ICT can most enhance teaching and learning in subject areas:
  - using data and information sources
  - searching and reflecting
  - organizing and investigating
  - analysing and automating processes
  - models and modelling
  - control and monitoring
  - fitness for purpose
  - refining and presenting information
  - communicating
  - reviewing, modifying and evaluating work as it progresses is vital throughout (this is one of the four themes of the National Curriculum programmes of study for ICT, the others being

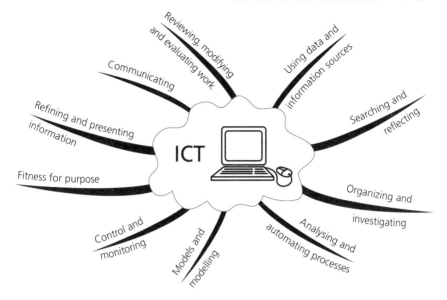

The 10 key ICT concepts

Finding things out; Developing ideas and making things happen; and Exchanging and sharing information).

- The degree to which you are able to take advantage of ICT in your classroom will depend on the hardware and software which is available to you, especially the availability of PCs or laptops.
- It will also depend on the vision and commitment of the school middle and senior leaders, who have a vital role in setting the tone for the use of ICT in specific subjects – this may be why there is as much variation *within* schools as *between* them, when considering how successfully ICT is used in specific subjects.
- All schools need to be careful that teachers not only use ICT themselves to aid their teaching, but that they also allow learners hands-on access to hardware and software to aid their learning.
- It's vital to bear in mind that many learners will be more familiar with using particular hardware (e.g. digital cameras) and software (e.g. Microsoft programs) than their teachers – what learners need help with is how to use the ICT to enhance learning within specific subjects.
- The government has no targets for how much or how frequently ICT is used by learners – more important is the impact that the

technology has on their learning. Learners will happily surf the net for a whole lesson, but how much have they really *learnt* from this?

Ask yourself

1 To what extent do you currently use ICT in the subject(s) you teach?

2 How do you use ICT specifically to aid your teaching?

3 How do your learners use ICT to aid their learning?

4 What are the barriers to your own and your learners' use of ICT? How might these barriers be overcome?

✓ To do list

☐ Carry out an audit of your current use of ICT in the subject(s) you teach.

☐ Study carefully the DfES ICTAC subject guidance (see below) and devise an action plan for improving your provision.

☐ Use your learners' existing ICT skills to enhance teaching and learning within your subject area – many learners are familiar with hardware and software which can enrich curriculum delivery, even if your own ICT skills are not well developed.

Want to find out more?

A range of publications is coming onto the market aimed at improving the use of ICT in particular subject areas. Network Continuum Press (www.networkcontinuum.co.uk) is a leader in this field.

Davitt, J. (2005) *New Tools for Learning: Accelerated Learning Meets ICT.* Network Continuum Press.

ICT Across the Curriculum

Embedding ICT @ Secondary support materials (www.standards.dfes.gov.uk/keystage3/respub/ictac)

• Extremely useful DfES packs covering 12 national curriculum subjects, with guidance on how to use ICT in the classroom to enhance teaching and learning. Each pack contains subject-specific advice, general guidance, software reviews and example lessons, with the aim of helping subject teachers to have a clearer understanding as to when and how they can embed ICT in their subject teaching.

ICT register (www.ict-register.net)
- A unique database, capturing ICT and eLearning expertise in schools and learning centres across the world. The database provides easy access to support and guidance from classroom practitioners who have already experienced the ICT issues which many schools are now facing. Services include telephone and email advice, visits, courses and audit procedures.

See also . . .

→✤ Accelerated learning, page 5.
→✤ Active learning, page 9.
→✤ Learning preferences, page 86.

20

Inclusion

What is it?

Inclusion encompasses the concepts of equality of opportunity and equal access for all learners in schools. If a school is fully inclusive every child or young person in its care, irrespective of gender, ability, race, ethnic or cultural background or other factors, is able to enjoy the full spectrum of opportunities offered by the school in order to reach his or her potential.

Knowledge bank

- The modern understanding of inclusion is a much broader concept than is often recognized by teachers. It goes *far beyond* work with learners who have special educational needs, which the concept grew out of.
- For schools to be able to declare honestly that they are inclusive they need to be prepared to work at the whole school *and* the

classroom level. Even then, being inclusive is more about a process than an end point.

- There has been a move in recent years to educate as many children as possible in mainstream schools, unless their needs mean that this is impractical. This has required teachers to respond to an ever more diverse population within their classrooms.
- A central tool to address inclusion is to identify potential *barriers to progress*. These are factors that may be preventing a child or young person from achieving his or her potential. They could include behavioural factors, a disability or learning difference, a language barrier, a cultural difference, or a whole raft of other factors.
- Once barriers have been identified, measures can be introduced that will allow you to help learners overcome them – these come in many forms and guises. Key to success is working fully *with* the child or young person.
- The successful inclusion of a child or young person into a school comes about through an effective partnership between that person, his or her parents/guardians and the teacher and leaders at the school. If one of these parties is not committed to the process, then it's likely to be an uphill struggle.
- Inclusion is most effective when it is supported at a whole school as well as a classroom level. While there are many things that individual teachers can do in their classrooms, these are not likely to have the desired impact if teachers are working within a whole school climate that does not cherish inclusion.
- Classroom teachers striving to become more inclusive in their work should begin by clarifying what an inclusive classroom would look like. The next step is to identify potential barriers to progress for individual learners, followed by implementing measures to try to ensure that these barriers do not prevent any individual from reaching his or her potential. Finally, these measures need to be reviewed at regular intervals.
- Becoming a more inclusive classroom teacher requires you to think about the inclusivity of your classroom layout, resources used and teaching and learning techniques. All these factors can provide barriers to progress for individual learners.

- A further tool that can be used to plan and implement actions for particular learners is the *Individual Education Plan* (IEP). This document helps to clarify potential barriers to learning and sets out what the school and others will do to help the learner to thrive.
- Teaching assistants can be used very effectively in classrooms in order to enhance inclusion – from working with individual learners to adapting materials or instructions in a way that makes them more accessible for key groups.

Ask yourself

1 How inclusive is your classroom? What criteria are you using to come to this judgement?
2 What can you do in order to ensure that you embrace inclusion issues as you plan lessons, teach and give learners feedback on work?
3 To what extent has your school developed an up-to-date view of inclusion, that goes beyond the simplicities of the past?

✓ To do list

☐ Write out your definition of what inclusion means to you in the context of your classroom.

☐ Identify the challenges that exist in embracing inclusion in the subject(s) you teach. Share this with your school's inclusion coordinator.

☐ Consider what other professionals working in your school can offer to help you make your classroom more inclusive – for example, teaching assistants, learning mentors, support staff.

Want to find out more?

Booth, T. & Ainscow, M. (2002) *Index for Inclusion: developing learning and participation in schools.* Centre for Studies on Inclusive Education.

Elliot, N., Doxey, E. & Stephenson, V. (2004) *The Inclusion Pocketbook.* Teachers' Pocketbooks.

Ofsted (2000) *Evaluating Educational Inclusion: Guidance for Inspectors and Schools.* Ofsted.

See also . . .

→❖ Differentiation, page 38.
→❖ Gender awareness, page 60.
→❖ More able learners, page 122.
→❖ Multicultural awareness, page 126.

21

Independent learning

What is it?

Independent learning is a process and a way of thinking in education within which learners develop knowledge, skills and understanding through their own efforts. The process supports the development of self-evaluation and self-motivation.

Knowledge bank

- Independent learning is also referred to as self-directed learning and encourages learners to accept *personal responsibility* for their learning.
- It is the preferred method of learning in universities and it greatly benefits learners if they can have had experience of this approach to learning before they attend a university.
- It benefits learners through:
  - a more adult and realistic approach to learning which reflects lifelong learning models

- the development of flexibility and good decision-making
- skills which can be transferred to other sectors and carried through life
- scope for different learning styles to be accommodated where choice is given over how to access sources of information
- greater levels of self-motivation through freedoms and choices.

- It is characterized by learners:
  - taking responsibility for setting their own learning goals
  - understanding how they prefer to learn and utilizing and extending their repertoire
  - planning and organizing themselves and their work
  - communicating ideas in a wide range of formats
  - learning though experiential processes
  - identifying and solving problems
  - thinking creatively
  - learning the skills of self-evaluation and relating their progress to their starting goals.

- In the school context independent learning has key relevance too. However, the challenge for some teachers can be to let go of their control and become a *facilitator* of learning rather than an 'in-putter' of facts. Judging when to help directly and how much help to give is key.

- An independent learning approach requires early *support* for learners in developing the key skills that it demands. This early development can then be allowed to flourish within the framework of support offered to the learners within the context of their independent working. Getting the intervention balance right takes time, and this can be helped by gaining learner feedback around the feelings they have during the learning experience, and what they would like more or less of from their teacher.

- Special emphasis on developing *reflectivity* for self-evaluation is essential in independent learning situations. Learners need to be encouraged to reflect not just on what they have learned, but also how they have learned it, so that they can improve their own learning effectiveness. This should be built into their planning.

- A level of *interactivity* with other learners, teachers and other adults is required in successful independent learning. To this end individual, pair and collaborative group work is necessary.
- Resource implications need to be considered and in particular:
  - Liaising with library/resource centre staff in relation to sources of information, space and support.
  - Training in internet use may be necessary.
  - Re-organization of the classroom environment to make it more appropriate for a flexible learning set-up. In some cases re-rooming may be possible permanently or temporarily.
  - Resources may be available beyond the institution, e.g. local industry, community. If so consideration as to how these will be accessed is required.
  - The implications for storage and retrieval of support materials and differentiated learning materials will need to be explored.
  - How you will distribute your time and meet your learners' needs.
- It's worth bearing in mind that independent learning need not require a wholesale shift, and that it can be developed and used within the context of a range of other processes and philosophies of learning.
- The learning that takes place in schools can never be truly independent since the role of schools is to provide teachers as expert facilitators or mediators of learning.

Ask yourself

1 What are your current feelings about independent learning approaches?
2 In what ways are you able to adopt these approaches?
3 What might be stopping you from taking this forward?
4 What could you do to develop your own independent learning approaches?

✓ To do list

☐ Find out what your learners feel about independent learning.

☐ Consider alongside your learners what kinds of principles and rules would be needed for independent learning to operate effectively.

☐ Investigate the resource implications of moving further towards this approach and consider ways to overcome the challenges.

Want to find out more?

Marshall, L. and Rowland, F. (1993) *A Guide to Learning Independently.* Open University Press.

Featherstone, S. & Bayley, R. (2003) *We Can Do It!: Practical Foundations for Independent Learning (Early Years Library).* Featherstone Education Ltd.

See also . . .

→❖ Active learning, page 9.

→❖ Differentiation, page 38.

→❖ More able learners, page 122.

→❖ Personalization in education, page 146.

22

Learning preferences

What are they?

Learning preferences encompass a wide range of models for explaining the variety of approaches that people adopt to learn.

Knowledge bank

- Over the last 40 years or so there have been a wide range of attempts to characterize the different ways in which people learn.
- These approaches take a variety of views – some suggest structural differences in neural connections within the brain, others are more psychological in nature, and the nature–nurture debate exists in all cases.
- The table opposite summarizes just *some* of the models and rationales that exist to explain differences in the way people learn.

Approach	Origin and rationale
Sensory preferences	Proposed by Grinder and Bandler, the originators of →✦ **Neuro-linguistic programming**, page 136. Originally they suggested that we have five sensory filters through which we make sense of the world around us: Visual (V), Auditory (A), Kinaesthetic (K), Olfactory (O) and Gustatory (G). This was simplified within educational circles to three, i.e. V, A and K. A later, and unfortunate, extrapolation of these filters to suggest they were a kind of learning style occurred. In this incarnation it was suggested that they were somehow fixed and discrete. This is far from the originators' intention. Nonetheless, VAK has become a simple and useful way to differentiate and provide variety of sensory stimulus in schools.
Information-processing preferences	A variety of writers have worked in this area, including Honey and Mumford and Gregorc. They have proposed models for the ways in which people process new information. Honey and Mumford's model consists of four styles of learning: 1. *The Pragmatist* who likes to think about how to apply learning in reality and real-life problem-solving. 2. *The Activist* who likes to get on and do activities like brain storming, group work and puzzle solving. 3. *The Reflector* who likes time out to consider, reflect and postulate before taking action. 4. *The Theorist* who needs models, frameworks, stories and statistics. Gregorc's model for learning preferences consists of four types: 1. *Concrete sequential* – learners prefer direct, hands-on experience, highly organized, sequential lessons, concrete materials and step-by-step instructions. 2. *Concrete random* – learners use an experimental, trial and error approach, have 'flashes of insight' and make 'intuitive leaps'. 3. *Abstract sequential* – learners like written and verbal symbols, often think in 'conceptual pictures'. 4. *Abstract random* – learners prefer to receive information in an unstructured manner, enjoy group discussion, cooperative learning, and multi-sensory experiences. There are, of course, overlaps between many of these preference models.
Intelligence	Intelligence approaches to learner preference often utilize Howard Gardner's multiple intelligence theory which holds that there are at least eight different types of intelligence. This has been developed by educators into a system for valuing learner difference, building self-esteem and providing activities and experiences within the classroom which meet a range of intelligence preferences. Note that it was not Gardner's intention for his intelligence theory to be used to categorize different types of learners; for more information see →✦ **Multiple intelligences**, page 129.
Relative lateralization	This approach, based on the work of Sperry, suggests that there might be differences in dominance within parts of the brain. The most well known of these differences is between the so-called left and right side of the brain. In this model it is suggested that the left hemisphere of the brain is responsible for managing logical and sequential processing, mathematical and scientific thinking, and that the right hemisphere of the brain is responsible for the intuitive, creative and pattern-seeking functions. More recent research using functional imaging techniques has shown this to be neurologically inaccurate, however it is still a useful psychological model for explaining simple differences in processing.

- In the final analysis all of these models have their uses in supporting us to provide for our learners, however there are still more approaches available and it is wise for a teacher to make their own sense of the models and find those that suit his or her own situation. Indeed, one might find that no *one* model suffices.

- With all models, it has to be emphasized that they are just that, models. They are not reality and are best fits. In this sense we urge caution in applying and using models with children, and in particular we urge caution in the judgements that are made from these models and what is communicated to learners. A popular perception has developed that children can be tested, categorized and even segregated and taught in groups according to a preference. This should be guarded against, as none of these theories are any more than suggestions of a learning preference. Indeed, it might be suggested that there is a little of each style in all of us, and that learning preferences change with experience.

- It is important to consider how your →✣ **Teaching style** (page 175) relates to the learning preferences of the children you work with. Many teachers find that their predominant teaching style is profoundly influenced by their own learning preferences and this can result in other preferences not being respected.

- In essence, these models can be useful for planning and reflecting and provide a framework for analysis when challenges emerge.

Ask yourself

1 Which learning preference models most resonate with you?
2 What framework for learning preferences are you currently using?
3 How might you use such models in times of challenge?
4 How could you use such models to inform your reflective practice?
5 How could your own learning preferences support and hinder the learning of your learners?

✓ To do list

☐ Decide which models of preference you will adopt in your classroom.

☐ Share the models you use with learners, simplifying the language where appropriate.

☐ Involve learners in considering how they are learning according to the adopted models.

☐ Encourage learners to be constructively critical of the use of models and frameworks as they consider how they learn and how they could improve their abilities to do so.

Want to find out more?

Ginnis, P. (2002) *The Teacher's Toolkit.* Crown House Publishing.

Smith, A. (1998) *Accelerated Learning in Practice.* Network Educational Press.

A useful introduction to learning preferences is available at http://ferl.becta.org.uk/display.cfm?printable=1&resID=7543

Dr Anthony Gregorc support site is at http://gregorc.com

See also . . .

→✤ Accelerated learning, page 5.

→✤ Differentiation, page 38.

→✤ Multiple intelligences, page 129.

→✤ Personalization in education, page 146.

→✤ Teaching style, page 175.

23

Literacy across the curriculum

What is it?

Literacy is the ability to read and write, a skill that has very significant influence on learners' access to learning and achievement across all areas of the curriculum.

Knowledge bank

- The introduction of the Literacy Hour in primary schools led to attention being focused on the way in which literacy skills could be developed through the students' secondary education.
- In the past the ongoing development of literacy skills was often felt to be the sole province of the English department. However, from the mid-1990s onwards there has been a growing recognition that throughout a school all staff should be aware of the way in which the whole school curriculum can be utilized to strengthen learners' literacy. It has increasingly been seen as part of teachers' professional duties to actively play a role in doing so.

- In 1997 the initial document of the DfES's National Literacy Strategy contained only a brief reference to the secondary sector stating:

   'Every secondary school should specialise in literacy and set targets for improvement in English. Similarly every teacher should contribute to promoting it. The principles for the management of literacy set out earlier apply as much to secondary schools as to primary schools. In shaping their plans it is essential that secondary schools do not see reading and writing as exclusively the province of a few teachers in the English and learning support departments.'

- However, concern regarding the low levels of achievement in secondary schools led in the academic year 1998–1999 to the DfES funding 22 pilot schemes in LEAs in England to develop strategies to tackle low literacy standards in the first years of secondary school. Lack of evidence at the end of the first year led to the project being extended. Work within these projects focused on extending the National Literacy framework to Key Stage 3, adapting the literacy hour to year 7, exploring the culture of the school as a literate community, developing effective catch-up programmes and providing literacy training for secondary teachers.

- By March 1999 the National Literacy Strategy planning materials showed that the DfES was starting to take on board the need for developing a whole school approach at secondary level and stated:

   'The National Literacy Strategy recognizes that literacy cannot be learnt in isolation. Reading and writing are essential across the curriculum. It is therefore important that the co-ordination of literacy planning, teaching and assessment is treated as a whole school issue. This commitment is seen as essential for all pupils whether or not they have been taking part in a summer literacy school, or are entering a Key Stage 3 intervention programme.' Extract from NLS planning materials for Key Stage 3, March 1999.

- In the intervening years individual schools worked on developing cross-curricular literacy strategies following the input of training and support provided by the Key Stage 3 Strategy. However, the Ofsted annual report of 2003–4 indicated that, while performance had begun to improve, there were still schools that were failing their students in this respect, reporting significant discrepancies between schools in the implementation of whole-school polices in this area.

- By 2004–5 they were reporting that only a minority of schools had built on the earlier work to develop effective approaches to teaching and learning in order to heighten the profile of literacy. In these schools they reported literacy as being regarded as a core element in lesson planning across the curriculum and as being supported by management systems that continue to value it and by additional whole-school activities that promote reading. Many other schools were regarded as still being in the early stages of development work, with yet others having policies in place but not applying them consistently. In schools of this sort they found that training had not been updated, reading and writing were narrow in range, and marking was not used effectively enough to support progress in writing across the curriculum.

- The report concluded that in order to ensure improvement, work needed to be done to ensure effective monitoring of literacy practice across the curriculum. They also concluded that literacy must continue to receive high status as a key element in all teaching and learning and that systems must be established to ensure effective sharing of good practice across all departments.

- At the National Literacy Trust secondary conferences of 2003 a list of essential ingredients for successfully introducing literacy across the curriculum was drawn up. These focused on eleven issues.

Successful Ingredients For Cross Curricular Literacy

1 The importance of developing shared aims with a clear focus and a clear progression to prevent taking on too much at one time. A whole-school approach to reading should be developed with this being seen as a priority.

2 Staff should be provided with time to embed approaches and there must be adequate provision of resources and admin support to allow this to happen.

3 SMART targets should be set for each department which are clearly related to whole-school objectives and which can be audited, evaluated and reviewed at regular intervals.

4 An effective, enthusiastic coordinator should be appointed within each school, supported by a high quality Local Authority or LA consultant.

5 It is important to build on primary practice – therefore a good working relationship with feeder primaries is essential. Curricular continuity is beneficial to learners.

6 Good practice should always be shared – peer observation is an especially helpful way to achieve this. If practicable this could be done across the feeder primaries and the secondary school.

7 Regular high quality training needs to be provided and effectively cascaded to engender confidence and enthusiasm.

8 Training must to be appropriate for the needs of different subject areas – recognizing that each subject area is different.

9 Literacy should also include a focus on speaking and listening as it is not something which occurs in isolation.

10 High expectations and positive reinforcement are required to achieve a sense of 'can do' within the learning community.

11 The whole school community needs to have a sense of ownership with regards to the literacy policy. As well as teachers and school leaders, it's important to involve learners, parents and governors.

Ask yourself

1 How do you currently try to develop literacy in the subject(s) you teach? What constitutes high quality writing in these subjects?

2 What resources do you already have/need to create to enhance this aspect of your teaching?

3 What barriers exist to your development of literacy skills within your subject and how might they be overcome?

4 How can you play your part in helping to deliver your school literacy goals? If you are not sure what these are, then there's some detective work to be done first! And if your school's leaders

can't identify these goals either, then there are some serious strategic issues for your school to wrestle with.

✓ To do list

☐ Prepare an audit of the methods you use to develop literacy in your classroom.

☐ Work with a like-minded colleague, who teaches a different subject to yourself, to produce a joint action plan for enhancing literacy in the subjects you both teach.

☐ Carry out steps to develop your own literacy through more varied reading and writing and by studying a professional text on the topic, relevant to the subject(s) you teach. Be aware as you do so that literacy skills do not necessarily have an end point – we are all continually developing these skills throughout life.

Want to find out more?

Strong, J. (2001) *Literacy Across the Curriculum: Making It Happen.* Collins Educational.

www.warwick.ac.uk/staff/D.J.Wray/fourroles.doc+literacy+across+the +secondary+school+curriculum
- Looks specifically at ways of developing literacy in science, English and maths.

www.warwick.ac.uk/staff/D.J.Wray/Articles/secondary.pdf
live.ofsted.gov.uk/publications/annualreport0405/
www.eriding.net/english/Secondary_resources
www.standards.dfes.gov.uk/primary/publications/literacy
www.standards.dfes.gov.uk/
www.nate.org.uk/
www.nla.org.uk
- The website of the National Literacy Association.

See also . . .

→❖ Oracy across the curriculum, page 142.
→❖ Writing frames/scaffolding, page 195.

24

Managing learners' behaviour

What is it?

Managing learners' behaviour is sometimes also referred to as 'behaviour management'. It is carried out in order to help learners become successful and achieve their potential. The key to behaviour improvement appears to lie in focusing not on improving poor behaviour but on promoting 'learning behaviour'.

Knowledge bank

- Behaviour management has become a key issue in many schools, with recent research by the DfES showing that school exclusions are on the rise, with a 6% increase compared to the previous year. Of these exclusions 30% are for persistent disruptive behaviour.
- Many behaviour improvement approaches focus on strategies but miss out an understanding of *why* learners misbehave. Without

this understanding teachers may be wrongly applying the techniques to situations which arise in schools.

- One of the principles of behaviour management is that if there is high-quality teaching and learning, then unhelpful behaviour will be much reduced – however, it will not disappear altogether, requiring teachers to think carefully about how they can manage behaviour.
- Knowing why learners misbehave and what causes them to behave appropriately supports the use of tools and techniques for behaviour improvement. Underpinning this approach to managing behaviour is an understanding of the neuro-science behind stress responses in humans.
- One approach to doing this seeks to describe the states of mind that learners experience in the classroom using a model called 'The Learning Zone Model' which identifies four different zones – essentially four states of mind that can impinge on learning.
- The zones consist of:
  - The Safe Zone: where learners feel a sense of safety, self-worth and physical and emotional security.
  - The Learning Zone: where learners are challenged and at the same time supported to learn.
  - The Anxiety Zone: where youngsters begin to experience negative stress about the learning experience, and low-level misbehaviour happens.
  - The Stress Zone: where learners react negatively in the classroom, are violent or uncontrollably abusive.
- This model seeks to give the teacher a proactive set of approaches to establish a Safe Zone, move learners in to the Learning Zone, recognize signs of the Anxiety Zone and equips teachers with tools to guide learners back to learning again. It also identifies the steps to take when learners stray into the Stress Zone.
- There are a series of principles which support this approach to managing behaviour, they are:
  1 Promote positive learning behaviours.
  2 Manage your own learning behaviours to manage those of your learners
  3 It's never personal.
  4 Encourage learners to take risks and support risk-taking.

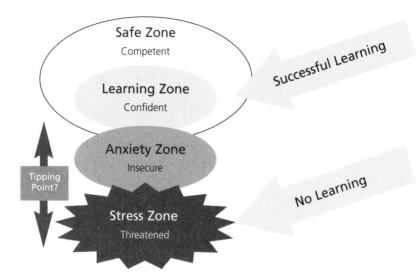

The Learning Zone Model: adapted from Lopley (2006)

5 Recognize that in crisis, learners need to go back to their Safe Zone before they can be in the Learning Zone again.

6 Children are more likely to behave if the lesson is engaging, varied and enjoyable: plan for it to be so.

7 Your expectations create your outcomes: focus on what you want, not what you don't want.

8 School is not the real world – take care not to take it too seriously.

9 Teacher self-reflection supports progress.

Ask yourself

1 How are you currently feeling about behaviour in your classroom?

2 What would you like to see improve?

3 What is currently getting in the way of high-quality learning?

✓ To do list

- ☐ Audit your current thinking and practice against the principles above. Identify the matches and mismatches here and make a note of the implications of your findings.
- ☐ Consider the Learning Zone Model above. How does it relate to your most challenging learners? Discuss the implications of this with a colleague.
- ☐ Consider to what extent good teaching is helping to establish good behaviour in your classroom. Create an action plan that will help to establish more positive behaviour management in your classroom.

Want to find out more?

Copley, A. (2006) *Challenging Behaviour: A Fresh Look At Promoting Positive Learning Behaviours*. Network Continuum Press.

Hook, P. & Vass, A. (2004) *Behaviour Management Pocketbook*. Teachers' Pocketbooks.

See also . . .

→❖ Accelerated learning, page 5.
→❖ Emotional intelligence, page 46.
→❖ Giving learners a voice, page 65.
→❖ Personalization in education, page 146.

25

Managing upwards

What is it?

Managing upwards is being proactive about supporting your line manager to do his or her job effectively, in supporting you to do yours properly. It involves building a positive rapport with your line manager, helping them to cope on a day-to-day basis and assertively stating your needs with regard to doing your own job.

Knowledge bank

- With increasing pressures on managers to be accountable it is not uncommon for a person in such a role to focus more on measuring success and on being seen to be active than supporting and delegating to staff they line manage.
- The result can be poor communication and insufficient awareness of the needs of their subordinates. Equally, managers can find

themselves overwhelmed with their role and may need particular support.

- There are four important factors to managing your manager effectively:
  - *Rapport* is key to the success of any relationship. Rapport can be defined as a mutual feeling of trust and a willingness to take risks. Taking time to build the relationship is key to getting another person on your side and having them communicate with you. Rapport is strongly improved by good listening. Even if your manager is not a good listener, modelling good listening for them may help to build a better relationship between you. In particular, as you listen to your manager, look out for clues about their fears and concerns. If you have needs and approaches you would like to see put in place, look at how you can tie these in with allaying your manager's fears and concerns. This also builds rapport, when your manager sees that you are responding to their concerns.
  - *Assertiveness* is when you behave in a fair, sensitive, respectful and optimistic manner towards others to put across your needs clearly and then stick to your request. It doesn't always get you what you want but it can be effective in influencing others, once they are clear about your needs.
  - *Willingness to support*. This is perhaps the most difficult area, particularly if your relationship is shaky to begin with! The key to this area is to put aside your thoughts of what your boss should or shouldn't be doing and to look at the whole department/school and the outcomes that are right for the children. Focusing on what needs to be done to support your line manager so that children get a good deal is essential.
  - *Posing challenging questions* is perhaps the most effective way to effect change and influence your line manager. Always to be done within the context of rapport, this will cause the individual to question their position on the area concerned. For example, what specifically will happen if we do what you have suggested? How do you know that you will get this outcome? What other possible outcomes could there be?

Ask yourself

1 Examine your own beliefs about your line manager and question any thoughts that bring up negative emotions or trigger defiant or competitive reactions. Could you find a buddy to help challenge these unhelpful thoughts?

2 Can you expand the range of challenging questions you ask, preferably open-style questions which encourage the individual to challenge their current position, e.g. What specifically do you mean? Always deliver this kind of question whilst in rapport.

3 Do you have the interests of your key stakeholders (learners and parents) at heart when managing upwards? This is where your manager ought to be focusing too.

✓ To do list

☐ Build rapport through mirroring body language and finding common interests both in and out of the work context.

☐ Use 'and' instead of 'but' when you need to disagree (e.g. I have listened to your ideas *and* I think we could also look at it from this perspective too – present your perspective followed by the benefits of this approach).

☐ In situations where your needs are not being met, decide what you need as a minimum in the situation you are in, and formulate the 'bottom line'. Communicate your needs clearly and succinctly and if they are not acknowledged or if they are refused, repeat them again and again using the 'broken record technique'. As a rule of thumb most people will listen if you do this clearly three times.

Want to find out more?

Thomas, W. & Smith, A. (2004) *Coaching Solutions.* Network Educational Press.

Knight, S. (1995) *An Introduction to NLP at Work.* Nicholas Brearley Publishing.

Pease, A. & Pease, B. (2004) *The Definitive Book of Body Language.* Orion Press.

See also . . .

→✤ Coaching, page 21.

→✤ Mentoring, page 110.

→✤ Neuro-linguistic programming, page 136.

26

Managing workload

What is it?

Managing workload is an approach to supporting you to achieve a healthy balance between your work and the rest of your life.

Knowledge bank

- Teachers in the maintained sector have on average 5.5 days off sick per year. Stress-related illness is the fourth official reason for teachers taking time off, but headteachers in one survey cited it as the number one reason. This points out the importance of managing work effectively to maintain health and well-being.
- Life–work balance is an important concept in managing your workload. It provides a rationale for adjusting your methods, practices and beliefs in relation to work. It encompasses an adjusting of your work patterns so that you find a rhythm which combines work with other aspirations and responsibilities.

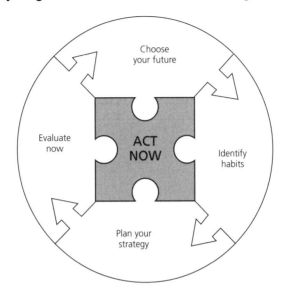

The Five Steps to manage your workload

- There are five steps involved in managing your workload:
  - Evaluating your current position – evaluating what's working and what is not working and in particular how satisfied you are with each aspect of your life.
  - Choosing your future by identifying in detail the kind of balance you would like in your life. This is about setting out a detailed ideal future.
  - Identifying habits that support you to achieve the balance you want, and those habits which prevent it occurring.
  - Planning your strategy to move you forwards towards your goals. This involves making an action plan as to how you will bring about your desired future.
  - Taking action to bring about change.
- Setting goals which are SMART is important:
  - *Specific* – state the goal with as much detail as possible.
  - *Measurable* – be clear about how you will ascertain when you have achieved it.
  - *Achievable* – ensure it is a goal which is something within your gift to change.
  - *Realistic* – make the timescale for change something manageable.

- *Timed* – put long-term timescales on your goals and also make interim timescales.
- Your goals should also be compelling and be connected to strong positive emotions for achieving them.
- An important element in taking control of your workload is to set up a *working envelope*. This is a contract which you make with yourself about the limits on time you'll spend working. This is important due to Parkinson's Law, which states that: 'work expands to fill the time you make available to it'. Therefore, creating a clear set of boundaries about how long you will work each week is critical.
- *Prioritizing* is a key habit to adopt and keeping a list of your priorities is helpful. Dividing the list into two columns headed 'important things' and 'unimportant things' is a useful way of deciding what to give time to and what to de-prioritize.
- *Organizing* your work space is important in terms of being effective with your time. Having a workspace which is clear and an efficient filing system (whether it's a filing cabinet or just a cardboard box divided up doesn't matter) is important. Organizing your paper filing and email folders, along with your 'my documents' folders so they all match, really helps you have an efficient system for filing and retrieval.
- Perhaps one of the most important habits to develop for most people struggling with their workload, is to say '*no*' to new tasks! But it's easier said than done. With proper prioritization and organization it *is* possible to be realistic and honest about what you can and cannot do for others. For some people saying 'no' is difficult. One simple approach that can help is to give yourself permission to 'say yes to saying no'.
- A key issue for many teachers is to improve the degree to which they delegate the responsibility for learning to their learners. Having learners working harder and teachers supporting them in this is ultimately better for their learning. This is especially true of →✢ **Marking** (page 107). Equipping learners to do more self- and peer-marking is both efficient for the teacher and also highly effective in terms of learning outcomes for the learners.

Ask yourself

1 How balanced are your work and life priorities currently?
2 What would you like your life–work balance to be like?
3 How could you take steps towards an even better balance? Who could support you as you move things forward?

✓ To do list

☐ Review your current situation. Consider the goals you would like to set for managing your workload.

☐ Get a supportive partner in your quest for a better balance, choosing a colleague or friend with whom you can have frank discussions and who could ask you challenging questions within a supportive approach.

☐ Attend a course to support your development in this area.

☐ Be prepared to challenge long-held beliefs about your work ethic and your approach to supporting others.

Want to find out more?

Thomas, W. (2005) *Managing Workload Pocketbook*. Teachers' Pocketbooks.

Best, B. & Thomas, W. (2007) *The Creative Teaching and Learning Toolkit*. Continuum International Publishing. Pay particular attention to the chapter on Teachers' Professional and Personal Domain.

Covey, S. (1989) *The Seven Habits of Highly Effective People*. Simon and Schuster.

For courses in managing workload visit
www.visionforlearning.co.uk/workload.htm

See also . . .

→❖ Emotional intelligence, page 46.
→❖ Managing upwards, page 99.
→❖ Self-evaluation, page 162.

27

Marking

What is it?

Marking might be defined quite literally as leaving ink marks on the page to respond to work done by a learner. Added to the ink marking has traditionally been the process of grading and commenting. Marking in its broadest sense is about responding to the learning experience of learners through feeding back.

Knowledge bank

- In recent years the traditional view of marking as a process of checking work for correctness and correcting issues has changed. Notably, the work of Black and Wiliam has challenged the value of ticks, grades and general platitudes (or in some cases, derision) applied to work by teachers.

- In 1996 Ofsted wrote that marking in secondary schools is 'usually conscientious but often fails to offer guidance on how work can be improved'. Black and Wiliam encouraged in its place marking within the context of supporting improvement and development, where the learner is at the centre of the process. Although →∗ **Assessment for learning** (page 13), as it has become known, is about much more than just marking, it highlighted four key areas for transforming formative assessment in classrooms, these are:

- *Questioning* – this includes putting more thought into framing high-quality open questions which promote higher-order thinking and increasing the amount of time learners have to think before answering.
- *Feedback through marking* – where teachers encourage learners to expand upon and show understanding of what they have learnt.
- *Peer and self-assessment using shared criteria* – where learners know what success looks like, and are taught the skills and attitudes of feedback and self-evaluation. Clear aims are required throughout so that learners can check back to see if they are meeting them.
- *The formative use of summative tests* – where learners are engaged in reflective activities to review their work and prepare revision strategies appropriately. They also suggest that learners should be engaged in the process of setting and answering questions about the learning they have experienced. They should also be able to apply criteria to understand how they could improve in future.

- Black and Wiliam explored the potential for marking to be truly *developmental* and challenged the value of summative grading and response in the learning process.
- Lovatt, Smith and Wise (2005) suggest that the term *marking* be replaced by *responding* and in their book outline a large bank of strategies for learner and teacher responding.

Ask yourself

1 In what ways are you currently making use of the process of formative feedback in lessons?

2 How could you further develop the culture of peer-to-peer formative feedback in your classrooms?

3 How are you using formative approaches to enhance learning and develop higher-level thinking skills?

4 How could you further develop a 'smarter not harder' ethos, through more learner-centred approaches to marking, while at the same time developing learner reflection?

✓ To do list

☐ Develop a protocol for feedback in your lessons, use it yourself and scaffold opportunities for learners to use it with themselves and one another.

☐ Study the excellent Assessment for Learning publication *Working Inside the Black Box* (Black & Wiliam 2002) which provides advice and strategies for developing formative assessment further.

☐ Find out what your learners currently find most helpful in terms of marking. Find out what they would find useful in helping them to develop ideas. Devise a short questionnaire to support your research and use it periodically to see how you are doing.

☐ Share good ideas on formative assessment with colleagues to build your strategy bank.

Want to find out more?

Black, P. & Wiliam, D. (1998) *Inside the Black Box*. Kings College.

Black, P. & Wiliam, D. (2002) *Working Inside the Black Box*. Kings College.

Black, P., Harrison, C., Lee, C., Marshall, B. & Wiliam, D. (2003) *Assessment for Learning: Putting It into Practice*. Open University Press.

Lovatt, M., Smith, A. & Wise, D. (2003) *Accelerated Learning: A User's Guide*. Network Educational Press.

See also . . .

→❖ Accelerated learning, page 5.

→❖ Assessment for learning, page 13.

→❖ Teaching style, page 175.

28

Mentoring

What is it?

Mentoring is a process of supporting others to develop through the provision of challenge, support, sharing relevant experiences and providing solutions.

Knowledge bank

- Mentoring, as distinct from coaching, provides support and challenge for an individual or group from a mentor who has experience and expertise in the field in which they are helping.
- Mentoring involves exploring perspectives, setting goals with the mentee and negotiating the agenda. The agenda for mentoring may well be set by the institution or might be more flexible.
- On the whole mentoring tends to be *provided* rather than sought and is typically used for new teachers, and for those growing into new roles within the profession. Additionally, mentoring is often

provided to learners who the school sees as needing support, i.e. they are in a particular group such as the C/D borderline.

- Although mentoring is traditionally an advice-based helping process it is often combined with coaching and even counselling skills (see also →❖ **Coaching**, page 21). In this way a blended approach to support is offered.
- *Mentoring* can be seen as the provision of advice, guidance and suggested solutions; *coaching* as the unblocking of attitudes and empowerment; and *counselling* as exploring and acknowledging emotional responses to situations.
- One model of mentoring suggests a three-step process (Garvey & Langridge 2003):
  1 *Exploration* – where the mentor takes the lead, develops the relationship, clarifies the objectives and negotiates the agenda.
  2 *New understanding* – where the mentor listens and challenges, gives feedback, demonstrates skills and provides information and advice.
  3 *Action planning* – where the mentor examines options for action, negotiates and agrees action plans and monitors progress and outcomes.
- The power relationship in mentoring is different to that of coaching. In mentoring there is a power difference created by the expectation that the mentor is experienced and has answers to problems. This can be efficient and effective in the early stages of a teaching career or in situations where individuals need direct suggestions to make progress.
- Schools that offer mentoring to colleagues, parents or learners need to have clear policies in place to ensure the consistency and effectiveness of the process. A key element of this will be to evaluate (usually through questionnaires) the impact of the mentoring that has taken place.

Ask yourself

1 How effective is the mentoring process in your school?
2 How are mentors chosen, trained and monitored?
3 How aware are people involved in helping others in one-to-one relationships of the differences between coaching and mentoring and to what extent do they blend the processes?

4 What are your strengths as a one-to-one supporter of learning? What areas do you need to develop?

✓ To do list

☐ Consider this briefing on mentoring and that of →❖ **Coaching** (page 21). How would you characterize the support you offer to, a. colleagues b. learners c. parents?

☐ Seek permission to tape mentoring sessions and listen to your interactions with the mentee after the session. What are the strengths of your intervention? What would you change? How will you make those changes?

☐ Appraise your skills using the tape and seek further support from colleagues, by engaging in learning conversations about supporting others.

☐ Consider and plan your CPD needs in relation to mentoring and coaching for the coming year.

Want to find out more?

Carr, N., Hermann, N. & Harris, D (2005) *Mentoring, Coaching and Collaboration.* ASCD.

Garvey, B. & Langridge, K. (2003) *Mentoring in Schools.* Teachers' Pocketbooks.

Thomas, W. & Smith, A. (2004) *Coaching Solutions: Practical Approaches to Improving Performance in Education.* Network Educational Press.

Courses are available at www.visionforlearning.co.uk/coaching

See also . . .

→❖ Coaching, page 21.

→❖ Continuing professional development, page 31.

→❖ Self-evaluation, page 162.

29

Metaphor

What is it?

Metaphor is a way of delivering messages in classrooms, assemblies and in conversations which involves using analogies or stories. It can also be used to develop ideas and solutions in a problem-solving scenario. Using commonly experienced analogies can assist individuals and groups to understand complex ideas.

Knowledge bank

- *Metaphors* are useful because they build a bridge between uncertain or complex ideas and that which is already familiar. Metaphors can come from teachers or from learners and can help to both put across ideas and also resolve problems. Metaphor can take various forms, each having its own power.
- *Comparisons* draw analogies between the real content you wish to get over and some life situation that everyone can relate to.

For example, if you wanted to explain to a group of managers how you wanted your team to develop away from a traditional top-down model, you could use the analogies below.

> *Sometimes teams are like an orchestra, kept under the strict control of the conductor. Each member is highly skilled but is able to do only what the conductor directs them to do, using the score the composer has prepared. What I am looking for is a jazz band – each member is highly skilled, yet they work together without constant direction, creating something new and each learning from the experience. What we have in common are a set of principles and goals that we will decide together so we know what key we are playing in and the style we want to adopt, and how long we will play for. That way we can improvise and make great music, bringing our own personality to it each time.*

- *Stories* draw on a familiar set of archetypes and formulae to appeal to the audience and to convey a message or content. They would typically have a beginning, a middle and an end.

The bear

> *A visitor to a zoo remarked to the bear keeper how sad a solitary brown bear looked, as it sat hunched in the corner of the bear enclosure. 'Why is the bear so sad looking? Is it because it is cooped up in the enclosure? Has it lost a cub? Is it unwell?' asked the visitor. 'No' said the bear keeper. 'He is perfectly well, and he has many healthy cubs inside the bear house over there, and the other bears are perfectly happy in this enclosure'. 'Aren't you worried that he is so unhappy?' said the visitor. 'No' said the bear keeper. 'I know exactly why he's unhappy'. Looking quizzical, the visitor replied, 'Really, why?'. 'Because he's sitting on a nail' said the zoo keeper in a quite matter-of-fact tone. 'That's bizarre, if it hurts him, why doesn't he get off the nail then?' asked the visitor. 'That's simple, because it isn't hurting enough!'. (From Best & Thomas (2007) The Creative Teaching and Learning Toolkit. Continuum.)*

- *Self-made metaphors* that another person develops are another method and this can be explored to help that person understand a situation better, or generate solutions for themselves. An example appears below.

  > *A learner says that they are 'bogged down by all their work'. The teacher replies by asking, 'What is it like to be bogged down?' Learner: 'It's like walking through thick, gloopy sludge and it's hard to move'. The teacher continues to explore the metaphor with the learner then asks: 'How are you able to climb out of the thick, gloopy sludge?' Learner: 'I need a strong stick and some sight of solid ground'. Teacher: 'Where will the strong stick come from, and where is the solid ground?' Learner: 'The stick is in the trees over there (points) and the solid ground is just in front of me.' The teacher then brings the learner back into the reality of the issue with 'So back to this difficulty you've been facing, what is the stick, really? Where is the solid ground?' Learner: 'The stick is my family, friends and teachers, and the solid ground is making a plan which I am going to do tonight.'*

- Working with a metaphor involves complex *higher-order thinking* to analyse and evaluate how it relates to real-life situations; it similarly involves *creative thinking* to embellish and picture the scenario. Considering a metaphor takes people into potentially quite deep states of relaxation and trance. In this way there are links between metaphor and trance induction in classrooms. In English language terms there are, of course, differences between metaphors and similes. In this briefing we have chosen not to make such distinctions, though you can do so if you wish. In our companion volume *The Creative Teaching and Learning Toolkit* we outline a tool for designing complex metaphors to deliver content.

Ask yourself

1 How are you currently using metaphor?
2 What kinds of metaphors do learners and colleagues currently use in conversation? For example, what kinds of analogies do they use in conversation?

3   Look at the most challenging areas for your learners or colleagues. How could metaphor be useful here?

✓ To do list

☐ Listen out for metaphors in your speech and that of others.

☐ Experiment with picking up the analogies that others use in their speech and asking questions to explore the metaphor further.

☐ Read a children's story book, such as a fairy tale, and notice how the author constructs a compelling storyline. Pay attention to characters, plot, dialogue and the underlying messages being communicated. Identify the key elements of the approach.

☐ Design a metaphor to deliver some content for a forthcoming topic or meeting.

Want to find out more?

Owen, N. (2001) *The Magic of Metaphor: 77 Stories for Teachers, Trainers & Thinkers*. Crown House Publishing.

Lawley, J. & Tomkins, P. (2003) *Metaphors in Mind: Transformation Through Symbolic Modelling*. Developing Company Press.

James, T. & Shephard, D. (2001) *Presenting Magically*. Crown House Publishing.

See also . . .

→✤ Creativity across the curriculum, page 35.

→✤ Hypnosis in education, page 69.

→✤ Literacy across the curriculum, page 90.

→✤ Questioning, page 155.

30

Mind
mapping

What is it?

Mind mapping is a way of representing and organizing thoughts in a radiant manner which fits with the associative way that memory and learning is constructed.

Knowledge bank

- Mind mapping has been around for many centuries as a way of recording and organizing thoughts. Indeed, Leonardo da Vinci was using a form of mind mapping in the sixteenth century and there is some evidence that they were even being used in the third century too. They have been developed and championed in the last 30 years by Tony Buzan, who has trade marked the term Mind Map.
- Mind mapping develops from radiant thinking. This is an associative process of developing ideas and connecting learning. For example, if you were doing a project on car design you might

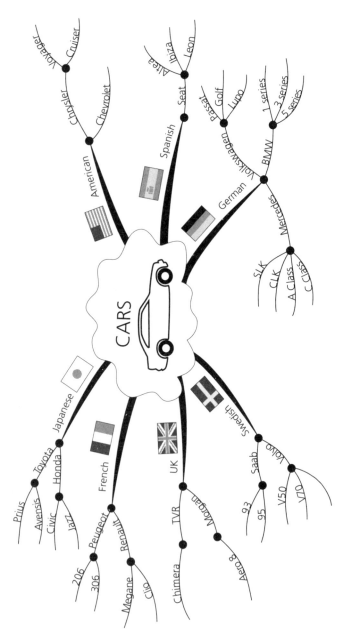

Example mind map on the theme of cars

start by thinking about cars, then notice what you associate with cars, perhaps wing mirrors, metal, then plastic and so on. Mind maps provide a way of visually recording and organizing this associative data.

- Mind maps are particularly useful for learners who are strongly intuitive thinkers or who favour visual methods of learning (see also →❖ **Learning preferences**, page 86).

- There is a series of simple steps to take to produce an effective mind map:
  - Start with a key word that represents the topic you're thinking about. Place this in the centre of a blank sheet of paper and add an image which you associate with this word.
  - Draw lines radiating from this central image and write words along the lines which you associate with the central idea. Add images alongside these words and use colour to make them stand out, and be memorable.
  - If you draw to a halt, add several blank lines and leave them, for your mind to fill later.
  - Take each idea, which you have developed from the central theme, and add further lines to this and write down words you associate with this theme too. You are now building a second level of association.
  - Once you have completed your map you can look for patterns and connections between ideas and you can if you wish redraw all or parts of it to emphasize the new learning you have gained.

- There are a wide range of benefits to making mind maps. They:
  - Promote creative thinking
  - Save you time
  - Help you communicate complex ideas
  - Aid your memory
  - Organize your thinking
  - Help you make new associations between ideas
  - Improve exam revision and hopefully performance!
  - Can help you learn more quickly and efficiently

- Some teachers shy away from teaching mind mapping to learners, because it is something they themselves don't find helpful. However, it is important to share a *variety* of learning approaches so that those with different preferences for learning can make appropriate choices.

- Although mind mapping has many benefits it is not the educational panacea suggested by some vociferous advocates. The key thing to appreciate is that mind maps serve their purpose, but are just one of a whole host of visual tools for organizing information and stimulating thinking.

Ask yourself

1 What opportunities are your learners currently given to work with alternative recording strategies to writing sentences?

2 How do you feel about teaching and using mind mapping? To what extent are your beliefs and preferences for learning influencing your views in this area (positively and negatively)?

3 What further support do you need to assist you in developing this as a technique in your classrooms or your own work?

✓ To do list

☐ Practise using mind maps for your own benefit for things like compiling shopping lists, resource lists, planning schemes of work and so forth. Also use them as interim stages in planning.

☐ Introduce them to your learners and set a series of easy tasks first, such as mapping their hobbies and interests, before moving this technique into work-based contexts.

☐ Mind maps are brought to life with colour. Provide learners with a range of coloured pens or pencils to help them animate and add interest to their maps.

☐ Ask learners to summarize a whole module of work as a map as you draw to the end of each unit.

Want to find out more?

Buzan, T. (2002). *How to Mind Map*. Thorsons.
Buzan, T. (2005) *Mind Maps for Kids: Max Your Memory and Concentration*. HarperCollins.

See also . . .

→❖ Accelerated learning, page 5.

→❖ Active learning, page 9.

→❖ Learning preferences, page 86.

31

More able learners

What are they?

More able learners are those who achieve, or have the ability to achieve, above average in any specific subject or domain compared with learners in the same year at their school. Such learners may be more able in National Curriculum subjects, as well as a whole range of domains which are termed 'non-traditional areas' (e.g. chess, public speaking, wood turning, working with animals etc.).

The government's gifted & talented strand of the Excellence in Cities (EiC) initiative has introduced two additional terms that define more able learners:

- *Gifted* – refers to learners who achieve significantly above average (or have the ability to be so) in one or more of the National Curriculum subjects other than art, performing arts or physical education.
- *Talented* – is reserved for those learners who achieve significantly above average (or have the ability to be so) in art, performing arts or physical education.

Note that this means, using the government's definition, that an individual learner can be both 'gifted' and 'talented'.

Knowledge bank

- There has been a lot of emphasis placed on the needs of more able learners in recent years, fuelled mainly by the high-profile and well-funded EiC programme.
- It's important to recognize, however, that teachers have, of course, always worked with more able, very able and exceptionally able children. The recent initiatives have simply served to focus the attention of schools on the needs of such learners.
- Within EiC areas schools were given funds to work with their more able learners, and have been required to identify a group of 5–10% of learners in *each year group* as the gifted & talented 'cohort'.
- As the identification exercise within EiC schools takes place at the school level, such learners can only be termed 'gifted' in the context of their school – they may not qualify as such in a neighbouring school. There is no currently accepted *absolute* measure of high ability that is used consistently across schools, or to create a standardized national register of more able learners.
- Schools outside EiC areas have had more flexibility in their work with more able learners, but *every* school must now ensure that learners, including those who are more able, are challenged and reach their potential. As such all schools are encouraged to keep a register of their most able learners and their provision for this group will come under the spotlight in Ofsted inspections.
- The various definitions often hide the fact that learners usually display *different* abilities in particular subjects or domains – they're not simply 'more able' at everything. It's therefore advisable to always specify a learner's ability, and avoid saying they're just 'gifted & talented'.
- It's important to recognize that children are individuals first and more able second. As with any other learners, they have individual strengths, weaknesses and preferences which need to be catered for.

- Schools' provision for more able learners is most effective where it is provided within the context of an inclusive education for *all* children, as every child has particular needs. Provision for more able learners shouldn't be seen as elitist, as there should be parallel programmes in place for other groups of children (e.g. less able, those with special education needs, traveller children etc.).
- Working effectively with more able learners in the classroom is about using differentiation and other strategies to ensure that learners are inspired, challenged and motivated in their learning. Such strategies include:
  - choosing an appropriate learning activity
  - increasing the complexity of the stimulus materials
  - increasing the challenge of the tasks undertaken
  - increasing the pace of study
  - increasing the depth of study
  - increasing the breadth of study
  - increasing the amount of independent learning.
- Teachers working with more able learners need to consider the above strategies, but recognize that a particular *blend* of these is appropriate for individual learners or groups, and this blend might vary according to the task in hand or how familiar learners are with the subject matter.
- Learners who are more able can also be *underachievers* (and so not readily display their ability; →✻ **Underachievement**, page 192) and can have *dual exceptionality* (they're more able but also have a learning, behavioural or physical disability or difference).

Ask yourself

1 Are you clear about what constitutes high ability in the subjects you teach?
2 Have you identified the different ability levels of the learners you teach?
3 How do you cater for more able learners in your classroom?
4 Which aspects of your work with more able learners need to be developed? How?

✓ To do list

☐ If you have not already done so, write out the qualities of a more able (top 50%) and a very able (top 10%) learner in the subject(s) you teach.

☐ Create a register of the more able learners you teach, making it clear which category they fall into (e.g. more able, very able).

☐ Prepare a portfolio of learners' work at different levels to provide concrete examples of high ability.

☐ Work with your school's gifted & talented coordinator to further enhance provision for more able learners, for example by carrying out curricular innovations or enrichment projects.

Want to find out more?

Best, B., Craven, S. & West, J. (2006) *The Gifted & Talented Coordinator's Handbook: Practical Strategies For Supporting More Able Students In Secondary Schools*. Optimus Publishing.

www.standards.dfes.gov.uk/giftedandtalented/
• The government's 'gifted & talented' website, containing further details of the various initiatives and other useful information.

www.nc.uk.net/gt/index.html
• The Qualification and Curriculum Alliance's guidance on teaching more able learners, including case studies in the 14–19-year-old range. Contains superb subject-specific information, including suggestions for how to challenge more able learners in the classroom.

See also . . .

→❖ Differentiation, page 38.
→❖ Inclusion, page 78.
→❖ Personalization in education, page 146.
→❖ Underachievement, page 192.

32

Multicultural awareness

What is it?

Multicultural awareness concerns the need for teachers and school leaders to be aware of the cultural issues that can affect learning, as well as learners' ability to access the curriculum. It also extends to preparing *all* young people to live in a multicultural society, both in Britain, and as global citizens.

Knowledge bank

- Multicultural awareness is currently undergoing something of a renaissance in our schools, mainly due to a number of factors residing outside education.
- Multicultural awareness has also attracted a fair degree of controversy. This has come predictably from far right groups who are ideologically opposed to a multicultural Britain. But it has also come from more mainstream groups in society who have

mistakenly labelled it as being driven by 'politically correct' motives.

- The most far sighted and inclusive view of multicultural awareness recognizes that *every* culture requires equal respect and recognition – including the prevailing culture in the catchment area of your school, even if this is not ethnically diverse.

- Schools in rural or mainly white areas have been criticized for not preparing young people to live in a multicultural Britain because they did not try to enrich the curriculum with resources, examples and case studies drawn from or representing other cultures than the prevailing one. This is not to say that they were expected to do this at the *expense* of the prevailing culture.

- It's vital that *all* learners are encouraged to recognize and celebrate their own cultural background and traditions – some may need some encouragement to do this, especially where there is mixed heritage.

- On a day-to-day basis, being aware of multicultural issues means that in planning and teaching lessons, and in giving feedback to learners on their work, you're mindful of the need to embrace different cultures and ethnic groups. For example it may mean that when discussing religious festivals, that you recognize that different individuals in your classes may not observe the same festivals. It may also mean that you're mindful of taboos and sensitive topics within different cultural groups, or indeed different ways of interacting with authority.

- Many publishers and other resource providers have been slow to recognize the need for images that are representative of Britain today. This can have a negative effect on any groups who do not see themselves represented.

- Many practical things can be done to show your respect for different cultures. On a simple level, being prepared to understand and celebrate the culture of others is an important principle that can be injected into your teaching.

- Multicultural awareness can be considered as part of a wider agenda to ensure that *diversity* in all its forms is recognized, valued and celebrated. It can be seen as part of a drive to engender more tolerance and respect for others, especially those who are different from ourselves.

Ask yourself

1 How does your school embrace multicultural issues? How does this impact on your classroom work?
2 What is your view on the degree to which you can embrace multicultural issues in the subject(s) you teach?
3 Think about your own cultural background. What is important to you about that background and how can this be translated to children and young people in a way that respects the fact that they may not share this background?

✓ To do list

☐ Write out your definition of what multicultural awareness means to you in the context of your classroom.
☐ Allow yourself to have some open reflection about any reservations you have concerning multicultural awareness in schools. Then share some of your thoughts with a trusted colleague to gain their perspective.
☐ Prepare a personal 'cultural heritage audit', outlining what matters to you about your own cultural background. Ask your learners to do the same and then use this as a basis for discussion.

Want to find out more?

Booth, T. Swann, W. Masterson M. & Potts, P. (1991) *Curricula for Diversity in Education (Learning for All)*. Routledge.
Clarke, P. & Siraj-Blatchford, J. (2000) *Supporting Identity, Diversity and Language in the Early Years*. Open University Press.
Potts, P. (1994) *Equality and Diversity In Education: National and International Contexts*. Routledge.

See also . . .

→✥ Inclusion, page 78.
→✥ Personalization in education page 146.

Multiple intelligences

What are they?

Multiple intelligences theory is a view of intelligence that extends beyond that measured by traditional IQ tests. It encompasses a range of capabilities which include physical, intellectual and social aptitudes. The concept was developed by US psychologist Howard Gardner.

Knowledge bank

- Howard Gardner viewed intelligence as 'the capacity to solve problems or to fashion products that are valued in one or more cultural setting' (Gardner & Hatch 1989). He used a set of criteria to decide whether a capacity was truly an intelligence, which included support from psychological and psychometric test data.
- There is some dispute as to the validity of the application of these criteria and the judgement process has been described as more of

an art than a science. Nonetheless, Gardner's work has found significant favour in educational settings in USA and UK.

- Gardner initially formulated a list of seven intelligences. Intelligences 4 and 5 are ones traditionally valued in schools:

  1 **Spatial intelligence** involves the ability to recognize and use space in open and more confined areas. It includes the potential to manipulate 3D representations in our minds and relate them to reality.

  2 **Musical intelligence** involves skill in the performance and creation of musical patterns. It is characterized by the ability to recognize and compose musical pitch, rhythms and tone.

  3 **Bodily-kinesthetic intelligence** entails the potential of using whole body or parts of the body to meet challenges. It is the ability to coordinate body movements through a brain–body relationship.

  4 **Linguistic intelligence** involves awareness of language and of spoken and written communication. It includes the ability to use language to express thoughts and feelings and for memory.

  5 **Logical-mathematical intelligence** consists of the potential to analyse problems logically and carry out mathematical calculations. This intelligence is associated with scientific and mathematical operations.

  6 **Interpersonal intelligence** is concerned with the capacity to understand the motivations and desires of others. It allows people to work effectively with others. Educators, salespeople, religious and politicians all need a well-developed interpersonal intelligence.

  7 **Intrapersonal intelligence** encompasses high levels of self-awareness in terms of hopes, fears, emotions and thoughts.

- Since 1983 when Gardner first outlined his seven intelligences he has added an eighth: **Naturalist intelligence.** This he characterizes as an ability to recognize, categorize and draw upon features of the natural world. Other intelligences have also been muted, but provide real challenges in relation to definition and measurement; these include spiritual intelligence, existential intelligence and moral intelligence.

- Another key element of multiple intelligences is that they are *modifiable*, that is that they can be improved through practice and reflection.

- Multiple intelligence theory has been strongly advocated by many educators. It has been applied by educational leaders and teachers to manage a range of issues in schools. In particular, it is used as a way of looking resourcefully at the range of abilities and gifts that learners have. Some schools are using the theory as a way of building self-esteem amongst learners. This is done through offering learners the intelligences as a way of valuing all of their abilities.

- The theory has also had its fair share of critics, especially in recent years, including some vociferous UK-based researchers who have cast doubt on the validity of the ideas and the potential of using them to raise the attainment of learners in school settings.

- The intelligences are also used in some schools as a way of differentiating learning tasks. It is possible to develop lesson plans which incorporate a range of activity over time which appeals to a range of intelligences. Choices of activity can also be offered.

- Inevitably Gardner's original ideas have been extrapolated and extended *beyond* his original intention, yet many schools find that there is real value to them in adopting a wider view of intelligence and diversity in classrooms. The theory offers a way of positively supporting that diversity in classrooms.

Ask yourself

1 How are you currently celebrating diversity in your classroom?

2 What tools are you using to actively promote self-esteem?

3 How might multiple intelligences support your work in building self-esteem and valuing diversity?

4 In what ways might multiple intelligences assist in bridging intelligence gaps?

✓ To do list

☐ Read more on the practical applications of the intelligences in the classroom (Smith (1998) is especially recommended).

☐ Look at the range of tasks and activities you currently use with your learners. Identify which tasks match which intelligences. This will give you an idea of the range of human intelligence you are currently matching in class. You can then use this audit to research further approaches that will bolster intelligence areas in which you currently offer fewer opportunities.

☐ You might like to consider exploring your own profile of intelligences using one of the many multiple intelligence tests available on the internet. Caution should always be exercised in this area as few of these tests are scientifically validated.

Want to find out more?

Gardner, H. (1993) *Frames of Mind: The Theory of Multiple Intelligences.* Fontana Press.

Gardner, H., Csikszentmihalyi, M. & Damon, W. (2001) *Good Work: Where Excellence and Ethics Meet.* Basic Books.

Gardner, H. & Hatch, T. (1989) Multiple intelligences go to school: educational implications of the theory of multiple intelligences. *Educational Researcher* 18(8), 4–9.

Smith, A. (1998) *Accelerated Learning in Practice.* Network Educational Press.

See also ...

→✣ Accelerated learning, page 5.

→✣ Differentiation, page 38.

→✣ Inclusion, page 78.

→✣ Learning preferences, page 86.

→✣ Personalization in education, page 146.

National Strategies for schools

What are they?

The National Strategies for schools are a series of high-profile government-backed programmes to promote reforms to the education system and what is taught in schools. They include:

- The Primary National Strategy – launched in 2003
- The National Literacy Strategy – launched in 1998 and now part of the Primary National Strategy
- The National Numeracy Strategy – launched in 1999 and now part of the Primary National Strategy
- The Key Stage 3 National Strategy – launched in 2000
- The Secondary National Strategy for School Improvement 2005–6 – launched in 2005
- Plus a range of smaller strategies dealing with specific subject areas – e.g. technology, languages.

Knowledge bank

- The National Strategies for schools have impacted on the work of teachers perhaps more than any other government initiative over the last five years – especially in primary schools.
- Teachers are now working under much more prescription about *what* they teach and even *how* they teach it than ever before – notably in literacy and numeracy – though there have been recent moves to allow more flexibility following something of a backlash from teachers.
- The National Strategies have, nevertheless, done much to help improve standards in schools, especially where whole schools have been committed to taking on board the principles – across the curriculum as well as in the more obvious areas.
- A key challenge for teachers is how to embrace the National Strategies – which have often come with statutory force – while still covering an appropriate curriculum and by teaching in ways that are in line with their own and their school's ethos and values.
- Secondary schools have been less influenced by the National Strategies, though targeted efforts at Key Stage 3 have been necessary and subject teachers have been required to consider the cross-curricular implications of the other strategies.
- One of the criticism of the strategies is that there have been rather too many of them, on top of a range of other new initiatives, projects and targets for schools to consider.
- A renewed Primary Framework for Literacy and Mathematics was launched in October 2006, updating and refreshing many of the materials in the original National Strategies.

Ask yourself

1 How do the National Strategies for schools impact on your day-to-day work in the classroom? Which has/have the most influence on your work?
2 In what ways do the National Strategies aid your work as a teacher? How can they hinder your work?

3 How easy is it for you to incorporate the principles and
practicalities of the National Strategies into your personal vision
for education? If there are conflicts how can they be resolved?

✓ To do list

☐ Ensure that you're fully familiar with the sections of the National
Strategy documents that refer most to your day-to-day work. You
cannot form informed opinions unless you understand the
contents of the documents and the implications for your
teaching.

☐ Learn how other teachers in similar circumstances to you are
making sense of the National Strategies in their schools. Identify
things you can try in your own classroom. Share your successes
with others.

☐ Draw up an action plan that will enable you to ensure that any
work to promote the National Strategies is in line with your
school's and your own personal philosophy for education.

Want to find out more?

Details on all the National Strategies for schools can be viewed at
the DfES Standards site at www.standards.dfes.gov.uk, with further
information available through www.teachernet.co.uk

See also . . .

→❖ ICT across the curriculum, page 73.
→❖ Literacy across the curriculum, page 90.
→❖ Numeracy across the curriculum, page 139.

Neuro-linguistic programming (NLP)

What is it?

NLP is the study of effective communication, thinking and behaviour. It provides a philosophy and a set of powerful tools to effect change in oneself and support others to do the same.

Knowledge bank

- NLP holds to the philosophy that we create enhanced external results by examining and changing what is within *ourselves*.
- NLP holds that what we perceive internally, is what we project outwards. Therefore if we change our internally constructed perceptions we change the reality we experience outside of ourselves.
- NLP holds that if we believe we're the cause of what happens around us, then we can take actions to bring about change. If however we believe that things are done to us and that we have no control over how we respond, we're at what is known as

'effect'. Being at effect is disempowering and limits peak performance.

- NLP presupposes and draws on our untapped inner resources.
- NLP is capable of:
  1 managing thoughts and feelings, bringing greater sense of order and control
  2 using the unconscious as well as the conscious mind
  3 helping you to create high levels of rapport with people, quickly
  4 increasing your level of awareness of others so you can respond more appropriately to them
  5 accelerating the learning process.
- The originators of NLP, Richard Bandler and John Grinder, modelled people who were high-level communicators in their various fields, including Virginia Satir, Milton Erickson and Alfred Korzybski. From their modelling projects they created generic models of linguistics and kinaesthetic tools to bring about change.
- Powerful language patterns are a key part of NLP. By paying attention to the specifics of the content and more especially the structure of language, we can empower others to achieve their goals.
- NLP has begun to gain a following among teachers because they are recognizing that its principles have important relevance for learners – when used effectively, NLP can be a powerful tool to help learners achieve their potential.

Ask yourself

1 Does NLP offer any insights that could enlighten what happens in your classroom?
2 What do you know of related fields that help you to see what NLP has to offer?
3 What type of language patterns do you use and what does this mean for your learners?

✓ To do list

☐ Examine your own philosophies in relation to the key points above.

☐ Consider attending a basic NLP training course.

☐ Identify the areas of NLP that you feel will particularly help you in the classroom and focus your reading on these.

☐ Think of a situation where you're currently facing a challenge. Consider how you might be projecting your internal thoughts onto the situation, mind-reading the other person. Consider the effect of the behaviours you're exhibiting based on your current projections.

Want to find out more?

Knight, S. (1995) *NLP at Work*. Nicholas Brealey Publishing.

Lewis, B. & Pucelik, F. (1990) *Magic of NLP Demystified*. Metamorphous Press.

Robbins, A. (2001) *Unlimited Power*. Pocket Books.

See also . . .

→❖ Accelerated learning, page 5.

→❖ Coaching, page 21.

→❖ Hypnosis in education, page 69.

→❖ Metaphor, page 113.

36

Numeracy across the curriculum

What is it?

Numeracy is the ability to understand numbers and calculations. It is recognized as one of the most important life skills learnt at school, alongside literacy and oracy (→❖ **Literacy across the curriculum**, page 90; →❖ **Oracy across the curriculum**, page 142).

Knowledge bank

- While most teachers have long recognized the importance of numeracy, the government has strengthened its position within primary and secondary schools through a range of initiatives and measures. The key initiative has been the National Numeracy Strategy (→❖ **National Strategies for schools**, page 133).
- The National Numeracy Strategy was launched in 1999 as a means of focusing teachers' and school leaders' attention on this critical aspect of education. It is now part of the Primary National

Strategy and the Key Stage 3 Strategy. Its implications now extend far beyond the primary sector, with teachers in secondary schools also being asked to help develop numeracy.

- A shift of thinking has taken place, so that *all* teachers are now seen as having a role to play in helping to develop learners' numeracy skills. It is, therefore, vital that teachers of all subjects identify ways to develop numeracy skills in a way that fits with the content of the curricula for the subject(s) they teach.
- Much guidance has been provided by the DfES to schools on how numeracy should be taught in the primary phase. Indeed, many teachers consider that there has been an overbearing prescription on how it is taught. Guidance on the cross-curricular aspects of numeracy is less extensive, though it is beginning to be addressed through a range of materials.
- For some learners numeracy is a source of anxiety and stress. Careful attention to supporting the learning of mathematical process, and awareness of limiting beliefs that learners may have about numeracy, is important. Introducing it through games can overcome the mental blocks experienced by some.

Ask yourself

1 How do you currently try to develop numeracy in the subject(s) you teach?
2 What challenges are there in developing numeracy in your classroom?
3 What can you learn from practice elsewhere in your school that could enable you to develop numeracy skills more systematically?

✓ To do list

☐ Consider in detail the principal ways in which numeracy relates to the subject(s) you teach. Draw a mind map or other graphic organizer to display this information and use it as an aide-memoire as you build on what you do.
☐ Attend a course to learn more about the subject-specific aspects of numeracy in your classroom.

☐ If you do not teach maths, team up with a maths teacher from your school in order to gain fresh perspectives on the opportunities to develop numeracy in your classroom. If you do, share your expertise with others.

☐ Invite your learners to look for the number-related aspects of each lesson.

Want to find out more?

Koshy, V. & Murray, J. (2002) *Unlocking Numeracy*. David Fulton Publishers.

Lawlor, G. (2006) *Understanding Maths: Basic Mathematics Explained*. Studymates.

Rees, J. (2002) *Fizz Buzz: 101 Spoken Numeracy Games Ideal for Mental Maths*. LDA.

Numeracy Strategy information is available at www.theteachernet.co.uk/numeracy

See also . . .

→✣ Literacy across the curriculum, page 90

→✣ National Strategies for schools, page 133.

37

Oracy across the curriculum

What is it?

Oracy can be defined as 'listening, speaking and spoken interaction'. The term 'oracy' was first coined in the 1960s as part of a research study into classroom talk by Andrew Wilkinson at Birmingham University which examined how individuals learn by talk, and particularly by working in small groups.

Knowledge bank

- There is growing evidence that children's learning might be enhanced by collaborative working and by allowing them to bring their own language into the classroom, using it to formulate questions, speculate and hypothesize about the curriculum.
- There's been a shift in teaching which has allowed learners to play a more active role in the classroom. This was highlighted by the National Oracy Project of 1987–1992, set up by the School Curriculum Development Council and administered by the National Curriculum Council.

- The aims of the National Oracy Project were to:
  - enhance the role of speech in the learning process at ages 5–16 by encouraging active learning (see →✣ **Active learning**, page 9)
  - develop the teaching of oral communication skills
  - develop methods of assessment of and through speech, including assessment for public examinations at 16+
  - improve learners' performance across the curriculum
  - enhance teachers' skills and practice
  - promote recognition of the value of oral work in schools and increase its use as a means of improving learning.
- This project was based on *action research* (see page 159) by teachers in their classrooms and focused attention on the previously somewhat neglected area of education concerned with opportunities for developing spoken language. It looked at the spoken interactions between learners and between staff and learners, how these were recorded and monitored and how they could be better managed to encourage the development of speaking and listening skills.
- The ideas explored in the National Oracy Project were later incorporated into the National Curriculum (England and Wales) as part of the English Curriculum strand 'Speaking and Listening'. Within this strand progression is characterized by:
  - increasing confidence and competence in adapting talk, using standard English as appropriate
  - development in the ability to listen with understanding
  - increasing participation in discussions.
- Within the Scottish age 5–14 curriculum guidelines oracy features in the English curriculum as two of the key strands, 'Talking' and 'Listening'. They're also referred to as key skills in other subjects, emphasizing that they're integral to the rounded educational development of the learner.
- Oracy shouldn't be something which 'just happens' in lessons. It must be an integral and explicit part of lesson planning, with opportunities created for a variety of oral activities within the subject.
- Talking should be regarded as a way of helping learners to sort out their thoughts and as the main means of social communication and interaction. Learners should be encouraged

to talk with peers, teachers and other adults. Contexts for talking should be varied and there should be a range of talking opportunities across the curriculum so that ideas may be linked across artificial subject divides.

- Learners should be actively encouraged to develop a growing awareness of the language appropriate to different audiences, purposes and situations. This includes learning the importance of effective talking through taking turns and listening to others; being aware of the need to be able to appraise the effectiveness of different forms of speech; and being given the opportunity to develop their own skills in speaking effectively (e.g. through presentations, performance and drama, →❖ **Drama across the curriculum**, page 42).

- To ensure a wide range of opportunities the Scottish guidelines suggest the following areas to focus on when creating activities which develop 'talk':
  - conveying information, instruction and directions
  - talking in groups
  - talking about experiences, feelings and opinions
  - talking about texts
  - audience awareness
  - knowledge about language.

- *Active listening* needs to be encouraged across the curriculum. It is not sufficient to assume that because a person is there and someone is speaking that the first person is actually listening! Learners need to be guided to listen for information and given opportunities to learn to respond on an individual, pair or group basis. The teacher needs to model such skills continually and emphasize the basics of good listening – eye contact, body language, use of questions etc.

- To ensure a wide range of opportunities the Scottish guidelines suggest the following areas to focus on when creating activities to develop 'listening':
  - listening for information, instruction and directions
  - listening in groups
  - listening in order to respond to texts
  - awareness of genre (type of text)
  - knowledge about language.

- The teaching of oracy skills shouldn't be regarded as something which occurs only in 'the literacy hour' or as part of a subject-specific strand. Communication is a key part of education and the development of oracy should be cross-curricular and inter-active.

Ask yourself

1 To what extent do you use the subject(s) you teach to develop oral skills? Do you feel oral work could play a greater role?

2 Do you offer opportunities for individual oral work, small group oral work, class oral work?

3 Who talks most in your classroom, you or your learners? Who listens most in your classroom, you or your learners?

4 What barriers exist to your development of oral work in your classroom? What barriers exist to your learners' use of oral skills in your classroom? How might they be overcome?

✓ To do list

☐ Plan to devote more time to oracy in a specific unit of work in the future.

☐ Reflect in detail about the opportunities for oracy across your school and work with like-minded colleagues to develop a collaborative approach.

☐ Carry out some further CPD linked to oracy so that a specific aspect of your current teaching can be enhanced.

Want to find out more?

Holderness, J.A. & Lalljee, B. (1998) *An Introduction to Oracy: Frameworks for Talk*. Continuum International Publishing.

See also . . .

→❖ Drama across the curriculum, page 42.
→❖ Literacy across the curriculum, page 90.
→❖ National Strategies for schools, page 133.

38

Personalization in education

What is it?

Personalization is the process of tailoring a particular service to meet the needs of the user. Within the context of a personalized education service, *personalized learning* equates to learning that respects the individual needs, aptitude, learning preferences and interests of learners – with the key aim of ensuring that every learner achieves the highest standards possible. It has relevance to whole-school issues (such as school structure) as well as classroom matters (for example →✣ **Teaching style**, page 175).

Knowledge bank

- Though there has been much government emphasis on the personalization of learning over the last year, the idea is not new and simply builds upon what teachers already do well.

- The current government drive to focus on personalized learning is not seen by the DfES as a new initiative – instead it is a mission to make best practice universal. It has clear links with the ethos of the →✣ **Every Child Matters** White Paper (page 53), which emphasizes the importance of progress for all learners, at the individual level.

- The goal of personalized learning is to ensure learners achieve their potential by working in a collaborative learning environment. It does not mean the same thing as *individualized learning*, where learners work in isolation from others.

- Personalization links with many core values of schools, including →✣ **Inclusion** (page 78), →✣ **Differentiation** (page 38) and high aspirations for all.

- Personalized learning has strong links with *constructivism*, which stresses the need for individual meaning making within the learning process.

- The DfES recognizes five components of personalization and separates these into an 'inner core' and the 'elements of personalising the learning experience' (see diagram). The most significant aspect for teachers is the inner core, which concerns classroom practice.

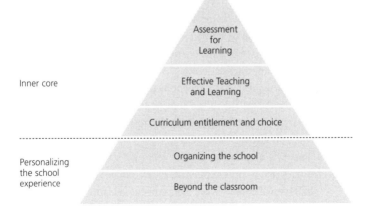

Components of the personalization of education, (DfES)

- The government will be encouraging and supporting schools to embrace the principles of personalized learning through a range of existing initiatives and strategies. It would like it to be seen as a philosophy designed to impact on all educational activity. It is supporting the work with substantial funding commitments.
- Schools are being encouraged to recognize that there are a whole host of partners with whom they should engage in order to get the best for each learner – they include parents/carers; the wider community (businesses and other providers of services locally); the local authority; the DfES and other schools.
- High-quality teaching and learning forms an essential component of personalization within schools, and teachers should ensure that learning experiences are tailored to the needs of individuals, not 'pitched at the middle'.
- Personalization is harder to achieve for learners who are very able or who struggle to access the curriculum for a range of reasons. Such groups will need special attention.
- Personalization can be seen as a banner for tackling a whole host of disparate issues which are important to the work of teachers.
- Achieving personalization can be seen as a seven-step process (see list below) – progress will need to be made on all these fronts if a school is to genuinely move forward.

Seven steps to personalized learning

1 Understand that the personalization agenda covers more than just one group of learners – it's about meeting the needs of *all* learners and represents the opportunity to enhance provision in an inclusive way.

2 Be clear about what is meant by personalization in the context of schools (the DfES's five components) and establish what your school is already doing to address personalization through audit/self-evaluation.

3 Integrate personalization with your own school's vision and values and recognize the links to related areas – differentiation, inclusion, high expectations for all etc.

4 Create an action plan to address personalization, spanning classroom, schoolwide and community priorities – ensure you have SMART targets and clarify the funds/resources to be committed to make things happen.

5 Blend classroom practice (assessment for learning, teaching and learning approaches, curriculum issues) and wider school/community approaches, learning from good practice elsewhere, to enhance opportunities for all learners.

6 Harness the support of key partners to help achieve personalization in your school – from parents to the local authority.

7 Monitor and evaluate progress against clear objectives and be flexible to new opportunities and committed to building effective partnerships to achieve greater success.

Ask yourself

1 What measures are *already* in place in your school and classroom to personalize learning?

2 What challenges remain at the classroom level as you try to embrace more fully the personalization agenda?

3 Which partners are worth working with in your local community in order to build a more powerful force for personalization at the classroom level? What specifically can these partners do?

✓ To do list

☐ Write a mission statement that makes clear what personalization means to you in a classroom context.

☐ Study the diagram which outlines the government's vision for personalized learning. Devise steps to tackle each of the elements in the 'inner core'.

☐ Discuss with your learners what personalization means to them – you may need to present the concept in a way that makes more sense to them.

Want to find out more?

West-Burnham, J. (2006) *Personalizing Learning: Transforming Education for Every Child.* Network Continuum Press.

Wilmst, E. (2006) *Personalising Learning in the Primary Classroom: A Practical Guide for Teachers and School Leaders*. Crown House Publishing.

The government's personalized learning website can be browsed at www.standards.dfes.gov.uk/personalisedlearning

See also . . .

→✤ Differentiation, page 38.
→✤ More able learners, page 122.
→✤ Streaming, setting, banding or mixed-ability teaching?, page 168.

Presenting skills

What are they?

Presenting skills are approaches to making maximum impact when introducing ideas to others.

Knowledge bank

- A presentation is a fast and potentially effective method of getting ideas across to others.
- It is a key skill which can be used effectively in the classroom, though should be used sparingly. It will also be required at many interviews, particularly for senior posts, and is necessary when pitching for projects or bidding for funding in the education market place.
- A really good presentation allows you to sell an idea or a service or in some cases yourself. Excellent presentations have certain key features in common:

- You look the part – you are dressed appropriately to build a relationship with your audience.
- You have crystal-clear objectives in terms of what you want to get across. A maximum of three key objectives is usually enough for a 30-minute presentation.
- You are well planned and have clear and well-thought-through points to make, and present reasoned arguments backed by data.
- If you are using a presentation system, such as PowerPoint, your slides should have impact through being succinct of word and visually stimulating.
- You come across clear, relaxed and confident.
- You build rapport with your audience by finding out as much as possible about them and their interests. Weave relevant stories and anecdotes into your presentation to catch and keep their attention. Make your opening remarks show that you understand their difficulties. You should give good eye contact and confident body language.
- You put your own personality into the presentation by sharing appropriate personal information.
- You allow people to ask questions, at the end of your presentation.

- Structuring a presentation is key. One way to do this is:
  - Connect to the problems the group face and to them as people.
  - Make the objective clear and deliver your key messages.
  - Exemplify your key points with stories, data and images, reiterating your key messages again.
  - Summarize again, verbally and visually, your key points.
  - Leave the audience with a poignant question or tap into their emotions through something appropriate but unexpected, such as a quote, story or poem.

- The 4MAT system can be a useful structure for presenting information to appeal to a wide-ranging audience. It consists of the four key questions:
  - What is it that you offer? Define the problem and the solution.
  - Why should the audience be interested? Give the reasons why they should take you seriously, providing data where possible.

- How does what you offer work? Give the processes and details of the steps involved.
- What if they were to go for the ideas/service you are offering? Outline the key benefits to adopting the approach you're suggesting.

- With all of the above in place it's time to deliver. Many people find themselves well prepared and rehearsed, but then nerves get the better of them. Having a ritual can work well as you step into the presenting arena. Here are some rituals that work well for some people. It's best if you develop one of your own:
  - Imagining a pool of golden light on the floor where you will stand. Picture yourself standing in the pool of golden light feeling great, relaxed and certain of your material. As it is your time to step up, step into the golden light and feel the warmth and calmness fill you. Pause, and then begin.
  - Before the presentation, imagine a time you felt really good, really calm and really successful, bring the feelings up that you had as you think about that time. When the feelings are strong and real, pinch your thumb and forefinger together on one hand to anchor the feelings. Repeat this with other remembered events and also when you naturally feel good. This will set up an anchor which you can fire off when you are about to present, by pressing your thumb and forefinger together. Anchors remind your brain how to feel good.
  - Have a set of affirmations or positive phrases that you say to yourself in your head before you present, e.g. I am an amazing presenter, I am confident and connect with my group easily and effortlessly. You may not believe this at first, but reinforcing this positive message over and again will bring forward the best in your abilities as a presenter.
- Above all else, set out to enjoy presenting, enjoy your message, be passionate, and be yourself, and your audience will love you!

Ask yourself

1 What are your successes as a presenter?
2 How are you currently doing with your presenting? What is working well and what would you like to change?

3 What are you currently saying to yourself as you prepare to present? Is it supportive or otherwise?

4 What steps might you need to take to improve your techniques further?

5 How can your presentation skills be used in the classroom context? What aspects are appropriate and what are challenges for classroom-based learning?

✓ To do list

☐ List your strengths as a presenter. Then video yourself in a presenting situation and get used to focusing on the things you do well as you watch it. Have a friend help you with this.

☐ Seek constructive feedback on your approaches to presenting.

☐ Take a course in presentation skills where you can have a safe opportunity to practise and receive tips.

☐ Consider seeking help with irrational fears about presenting, this could be from a coach, hypnotherapist or timeline therapist.

Want to find out more?

James, T. & Shepard, D. (2001) *Presenting Magically.* Crown House Publishing.

Professional support for training can be gained through info@visionforlearning.co.uk. This includes help with techniques for presenting and with fears and other negative emotions associated with presenting.

See also . . .

→✤ Metaphor, page 113.

40

Questioning

What is it?

Teachers pose *questions* of their learners in order to probe their understanding. There is quite an art to the process of effective questioning, and when used effectively, questioning can be a very powerful tool in a teacher's toolkit. *Higher-order questioning* involves teachers posing more challenging questions which help to develop *higher-order thinking skills.*

Knowledge bank

- Questions are an extremely valuable tool for any teacher, and can be used to clarify learners' understanding, prompt further thinking and help learners to mesh new knowledge into existing frameworks.
- A central point about questioning is the need for teachers to vary their questioning style, using a variety of formats including *closed* and *open* questions. In essence, open questions are those that

can be answered with 'yes' or 'no' responses – they tend to limit learner responses and thinking and should therefore be mixed with plenty of open ones.

Closed questions	Open questions
Did Hitler start the second world war?	What factors contributed to the start of the second world war?
Are the effects of natural hazards worse in poorer countries?	How do the effects of natural hazards vary between rich and poor countries?
Is Frank Lampard England's best mid-fielder?	What skills does Frank Lampard possess as a footballer and how do these compare to other players?
Is the computer the greatest invention in history?	How has the computer changed society and to what extent is it the finest invention ever created?
Was Shakespeare the finest playwright in English history?	To what extent can it be said that every major theme in English theatre was covered by Shakespeare's works?

- Do not forget that there *is* a place for closed questions, which can have a value in themselves, but that most of the questions you ask as a teacher should be open ones which really make learners think.

- There are important links between questioning and thinking skills in that questions can lead learners through different types of thinking, and if used effectively, can help to stimulate higher-order thinking.

- Encourage learners to use 'wait time' – at least ten seconds – before offering a response. This requires a culture shift in some classrooms, where traditionally learners have been encouraged to put their hands up, sometimes competitively, to answer a question as quickly as possible.

- Some schools take a radical stance and ban 'hands up', in favour of learners discussing among themselves a question and the teacher calling upon different pairs or individuals to offer a response.

- The Philosophy for Children approach provides an ideal way to ask meaningful questions of learners – its roots lie in the work of the ancient philosophers.

- Asking the right question can be an excellent way to solve a problem – help learners to practise framing insightful questions when they're stuck (see below).

Questions to get you out of a rut

What's causing me to choose to do things this way?
In what other ways could I approach this?
What blinkers am I wearing?
What assumptions am I making?
How could I change the way I'm thinking about this?
How would somebody else (e.g. an artist, musician, mathematician etc.) look at this?

Ask yourself

1 Reflect on the questioning techniques you currently use – to what extent do you use open questions?
2 What happens when you ask closed questions? – contrast the responses of your learners to situations when you ask more open questions.
3 In which situations do closed questions seem appropriate?

✓ To do list

☐ Be aware of the questioning techniques you're using as you teach – and strive to increase your repertoire over a period of time.
☐ Devise a plan that will enable you to use more open questions in your lessons and work with a colleague to embed this into your classrooms.
☐ Encourage learners to pose open questions of each other during the lesson.

Want to find out more?

Wragg, E.C. & Brown, G. (2001) *Questioning in the Secondary School*. Routledge Falmer.

Black, P., Harrison, C., Lee, C., Marshall, B. & Wiliam, D. (2003) *Assessment for Learning: Putting It into Practice.* Open University Press.

Cotton, K. (2000) *The Schooling Practices that Matter Most.* Northwest Regional Education Laboratory.

www.nwrel.org/scpd/sirs/3/cu5.html
• Useful web reference on Socratic questioning techniques for teachers.

www.sapere.net
• The website of the Philosophy for Children movement.

See also . . .

→✣ Teaching style, page 175.
→✣ Thinking skills, page 179.

41

Research in education

What is it?

Research in education seeks to discover patterns, trends and truths that can inform the work of teachers and school leaders. *Action research* is a specific type of research which is designed to provide insights that will enable an improvement in performance – in the case of education, usually more effective teaching and learning.

Knowledge bank

- Whereas medicine tends to be an evidence-based profession, relying on what we know tends to work, education has evolved a dynamic all of its own, which combines common-sense ideas on what works in the classroom with some findings from the world of research.
- This is actually a rather curious anomaly, given that over £20 billion is invested into schools in the UK every year by the

government. Many observers feel that we need to move towards education being based much more on evidence about what is successful.

- The analogy that is sometimes used is that teachers should become experts in learning, rather like doctors are experts in healing.
- The 'science' underpinning most research into learning is psychology, since in characterizing learning we are interested in analysing human behaviour.
- A key problem in translating what we know about learning into practical measures for the classroom is that the concept of 'proof' is much more elusive in psychology than in the purer sciences.
- The nature of human interaction, as manifested in activities such as teaching and learning, is so complex that it is very difficult to identify precisely which factors result in which outcomes.
- Instead of being able to show *conclusively* that a particular teaching method is successful at achieving specific intended outcomes, education researchers often talk about their research findings supporting an overall theory or paradigm for learning. These are usually underpinned by a leading figure in psychology who has written extensively in the field and has attracted a prominent following.
- The difficulty of using research findings to transform classroom practice is made even more challenging by the fact that few research studies are actually carried out in real classrooms. This is due to a variety of practical, ethical and financial reasons.
- Despite the above provisos, there *is* much we can learn from the world of education research that can illuminate what's happening in our classrooms and schools. In particular, there are many case studies and more rigorous experimental procedures that help illuminate the methods which are likely to be more successful.
- Education research lies on a spectrum from action research in a single school carried out by an individual teacher, to a large-scale standardized programme across many schools to test a particular method or approach. Most researchers accept that larger the scale of the study, the more likely it is to reveal generalized patterns that may be relevant in your own school.

Ask yourself

1 What education research are you aware of that informs your practice on a day-to-day basis?

2 To what extent is research in education important to you?

3 What questions about learning are you most curious to find the answers to?

✓ To do list

☐ Read more about a specific aspect of learning that interests you.

☐ Consider engaging in some action research in your own school.

☐ Attend a conference that allows you to make contact with some leading thinkers in the world of education research.

Want to find out more?

Petty, G. (2007) *Evidence-based Teaching*. Nelson Thornes.

Muijs, D. & Reynolds, D. (2005) *Effective Teaching: Evidence and Practice*. Paul Chapman Publishing.

Bell, J. (2001) *Doing Your Research Project*. Open University Press.

See also . . .

→❖ Enquiry-based learning, page 50.

→❖ Evidence-based teaching, page 57.

→❖ Self-evaluation, page 162.

42

Self-evaluation

What is it?

Self-evaluation is the process of auditing and making judgements about your professional performance for the purposes of improvement.

Knowledge bank

- Self-evaluation is just one of a range of ways in order to judge success and plan for improvement in schools. It is usually carried out by judging your performance against a series of criteria or standards.
- Self-evaluation can operate at a range of levels, from the whole school through individual subject areas to the work of a specific teacher.
- In recent years the government has formalized the process of self-evaluation in schools, through its new reporting procedures for Ofsted inspections. However, it's important to note that the

process is *not* simply another government initiative – self-evaluation in some shape or form has been embedded in many schools' (and other organizations') work for some time, and is widely recognized as a powerful tool for improvement.

- The spirit of self-evaluation in education is to encourage those working in the school to identify what is working well, while at the same time recognizing things that need attention in order for improvements to be made.

- One of the valuable features of self-evaluation is its ability to provide a baseline against which to judge future progress. The process can be carried out on several different dates, spaced out over a period of months or years, to obtain high-quality quantitative data. This can be analysed in order to pick out trends and patterns. Moving forward, things can then be reviewed at regular intervals, using the same self-evaluation framework.

- The principal value of self-evaluation to the day-to-day work of the classroom teacher is its ability to provide, in a focused way, a means of analysing in detail what is happening in classrooms and elsewhere, and the impact this is having on learners.

- The highest-quality self-evaluation at the classroom level occurs when teachers tailor the self-evaluation materials to their own specific circumstances.

- Self-evaluation requires openness and honesty on behalf of those taking part. An unfortunate feature of Ofsted's self-evaluation process is that the findings can be used as a stick with which to beat schools, rather than merely a genuine tool for school improvement. This has had an impact on the ability of schools to engage honestly with the process.

- The most effective teachers are involved in regular self-evaluation of their work and recognize the importance of this tool to hone their practice. This goes far beyond mere reflection by the teacher on lessons, though it grows out of such reflection.

- Teachers are likely to see the influence of their school's self-evaluation work through a range of new measures and changing emphases, including some which may become requirements in their classroom *against* their wishes.

Ask yourself

1 To what extent do you use self-evaluation in your work as a teacher?
2 How does your self-evaluation work relate to other aspects of your continuing professional development?
3 How does your school's self-evaluation work impact on you on a day-to-day basis?
4 Who else can support you as you engage in self-evaluation work of your own?

✓ To do list

☐ Find out more about the self-evaluation work taking place in your school, including the people responsible and the key documents relating to your institution.
☐ The companion volume to this book, *The Creative Teaching and Learning Toolkit,* contains a comprehensive self-evaluation tool designed to guide you through the Five Domains of Effective Teaching. You can use it to tailor your own development programme.
☐ Decide what specific aspects of your teaching should come under most scrutiny in your own self-evaluation work.

Want to find out more?

You can learn more about the Ofsted self-evaluation process at www.oftsed.gov.uk
MacBeath, J. & McLynn, A. (2002) *Self-evaluation: What's In It for Schools?* Routledge Falmer.
MacBeath, J. (2006) *The Self-Evaluation File*. Learning Files Scotland.

See also . . .

→✣ Evidence-based teaching, page 57.
→✣ Research in education, page 159.
→✣ Teaching style, page 175.

43

Starters and plenaries

What are they?

Starters and *plenaries* are beginning and ending activities which seek to connect learners to prior learning and review and consolidate learning respectively.

Knowledge bank

- The National Strategy initiatives (→ ✣ **National Strategies for schools**, page 133) have championed the use of active approaches to connecting learners to lesson content and reviewing learning experiences during a lesson before learners leave.
- Prior to this practice being enshrined in the National Strategies, accelerated-learning approaches were advocating this as a crucial practice in linking, consolidating and remembering learning.
- *Starters* have the following benefits:
  - They connect learners to the content and process of the lesson.

- They enable learners to make links between what they already know and what they are about to learn.
- They acknowledge prior knowledge and build self-esteem in this way.
- They actively engage learners within a short time of them beginning the lesson.
- They establish the expectation that the lesson is about engaged learning from the very start.

- *Plenaries* have the following benefits:
  - They allow learners to consolidate what has been learned.
  - They enable learners to reflect upon *how* they have learned and how they can improve their approach to learning.
  - They serve as a check back to the learning outcomes from the beginning of the lesson, to assess success and what else might need to be done to meet the aims.
  - They give an opportunity for learners to use memory tools to commit ideas to long-term memory.
  - They provide an opportunity to preview forthcoming learning and leave learners with questions to engage them for next time.

- The primacy and recency effect established through educational research studies suggests that we remember more about the starts and ends of learning experiences than we do about the middle. Similarly, the well-documented Ebbinghaus Curve of Forgetting suggests that without a summary to a learning experience we will forget around 60 per cent of what we have learnt within 24 hours. Such data is always open to interpretation, but it does add weight to the need for a plenary experience for learners.

- Activities for starters and plenaries can range from simple 'review three things you learnt last lesson' to more elaborate and multi-sensory approaches such as 'review in the style of a favourite celebrity what you have learned today' or 'here are five answers from the last lesson on this topic, now make up the questions to go with the answers'. In *The Creative Teaching and Learning Toolkit*, we provide a range of starter and plenary activities in the form of a bookmark which you can copy, cut out and keep handy in your planner.

Ask yourself

1 How often are you currently providing starter and plenary activities?

2 What are the challenges to including them? Why is it worthwhile persevering if you have had difficulties?

3 Which activities do learners most enjoy? What do they value most?

4 In what ways are your colleagues using starters and plenaries? What can you learn from their work?

✓ To do list

☐ Seek the views of your learners on starter and plenary activities they find most useful and enjoyable.

☐ Encourage your learners to develop suitable activities for the group and get the ideas laminated and up on the wall.

☐ Set the expectation that learners will review their previous lesson at the beginning – even if you're not there!

☐ Develop and collect from other colleagues a range of activities so that you can provide variety of approach over time to keep the momentum of starters and plenaries going.

☐ Task learners to challenge you if you do not leave enough time for a plenary. Get them to give you a five-minute warning.

Want to find out more?

Best, B. & Thomas, W. (2007) *The Creative Teaching and Learning Toolkit.* Continuum International Publishing.

Ginnis, P. (2002) *The Teachers' Toolkit.* Crown House Publishing.

Smith, A. (1998) *Accelerated Learning in Practice.* Network Educational Press.

For more information about the national strategies see www.teachernet.gov.uk/teachingandlearning

See also . . .

44

Streaming, setting, banding or mixed-ability teaching?

What are they?

Streaming is a radical model of school organization where children are placed into groups according to their ability and stay in these for most of their lessons. *Setting* occurs when children are placed in different groups for a particular subject, according to their ability in that subject, e.g. top, middle and lower set. *Banding* is similar to setting but children tend not to be so narrowly grouped. If children are not placed in streams, sets or bands, then they're taught in *mixed-ability* classes.

Knowledge bank

- As a classroom teacher you'll probably have little choice over whether your learners arrive at your lessons in streams, sets, bands or as mixed-ability groups – this is a decision that school or subject leaders tend to take.

- Despite usually having little choice over the ability groupings of your learners, it has major implications for your teaching.
- There are many myths that surround the issue of ability groupings in schools, and it's vital to adopt an open but critical stance to anything that you hear or read about the subject.
- The essential truth is that there is as yet *no convincing research evidence* to back up the claim that in general learners learn more effectively in one type of ability grouping over another – be wary of anybody who speaks in terms of absolutes in this highly complex area of teaching and learning.
- The research studies that have been carried out tend to point out the positive and negative aspects of the different approaches, but provide conflicting data on just which grouping method is most appropriate for the majority of learners.
- Whether learners are streamed, placed in sets or banded the result is that learners will learn within a class with a much narrower ability profile than if they were in a mixed-ability class – the table below summarizes the pros and cons of the two types of models.

Type of grouping	Advantages	Disadvantages
Streaming, setting, banding	– Learners are closer in ability level, enabling the teacher to pitch work more precisely – Differentiation is less of an issue – Learners can work swiftly through the curriculum, enabling more time for innovation – Can result in fewer interruptions due to inappropriate behaviour	– Learners in lower ability groups can miss the 'socializing effect' of brighter learners – Can reinforce stereotypes and labelling of learners – Can result in feelings of failure for those not in top sets – Relies on accurate assessment to place learners properly
Mixed-ability	– Learners can benefit from the views of other learners with different perspectives – Sends out an important message about being of equal worth – Encourages learners to work cooperatively with others in readiness for real life – There is some evidence that less able boys can have their performance enhanced by working with more able girls	– There is some evidence that particular types of learners may be held back by others in a mixed-ability class (e.g. bright girls who can be intimidated by boisterous boys) – Can be extremely challenging for the teacher if there is a very wide ability range

- It's likely that *individual* learners do benefit from being placed in a particular kind of ability grouping. There's evidence to suggest that bright girls may benefit from working in a top set alongside similar learners, but that weaker boys gain advantage from mixing with higher-ability learners as part of mixed-ability classes.
- Effective mixed-ability teaching is, however, extremely demanding of a teacher and is sure to really keep you on your toes!

Ask yourself

1 Reflect on how the learners you teach are currently grouped – what challenges does this bring?

2 How can you build on the advantages that this type of grouping brings and address the disadvantages?

3 What are your learners' views on the value of particular grouping arrangements?

✓ To do list

☐ Consider gaining some experience of working in a classroom which has a different grouping arrangement to your own (e.g. through observation, a placement or collaborative project) – this will be enriching, will help widen your teaching repertoire and will make you a more rounded teacher, also enhancing your promotion prospects.

☐ Experiment teaching small groups of learners arranged by ability within mixed-ability classes (e.g. blue table for more able learners, red table less able etc.).

☐ Read critically on the topic of ability groupings in order to come to your own view on what is appropriate for your school.

Want to find out more?

Tomlinson, C. (2004) *How to Differentiate Instruction in Mixed Ability Classrooms*. Prentice Hall.

See also . . .

→❖ Differentiation, page 38.

→❖ Inclusion, page 78.

→❖ More able learners, page 122.

→❖ Personalization in education, page 146.

→❖ Teaching style, page 175.

45

Target-setting approaches

What are they?

Target setting is the process of generating a specific outcome for oneself. It is characterized by a series of elements which make it both specific and trackable, but also emotionally motivating.

Knowledge bank

- Traditional target-setting approaches have centred around a process of deciding future grades or other quantitative measures. However, research tells us that the setting of compelling, effective targets is a complex process involving the following factors.
- Targets need to be SMART:
  - *Specific* – highly detailed
  - *Measurable* – ways built into it of quantifying the output
  - *Achievable* – the owner of the target has a sense of the end point being manageable

- *Relevant* – the owner of the target sees that the target is worth striving for, themselves
- *Trackable* – the target can be monitored at various checking points along the journey to the final output.

- *Ownership* is paramount. Formulation of targets needs to involve the individual, so that they have motivationally 'bought in' to the target.

- Targets appear more compelling for many people when there is an element of imagining a *future*, having already achieved the target. Inviting people to imagine a time in the future when they have already achieved the outcome can bring them in touch with the possible process for achieving the goal.

- Targets for many people are more compelling if they can include a sensory element in the outcome such as: seeing the finished outcome; hearing sounds linked to it; seeing statements about the completed objectives; and the feeling of emotions having successfully completed it.

- Once a goal has been formulated, it is also important to formulate *behavioural targets* too. In other words identifying the specific behaviours which will support achieving the target set. For example, asking good questions when we don't understand.

- Any more than five targets and it becomes more difficult to remember and articulate what your targets are. Creating *themes* of targets across a series of areas of the individual's work is a way of reducing the overall number of targets. This can maximize the chances of success, with fewer targets to focus on overall.

Ask yourself

1 To what extent are the targets set with your learners truly SMART?
2 How much ownership do your learners/colleagues have of their targets?
3 To what extent are targets reviewed and learning drawn from the experience?
4 To what extent are target-specific behaviours explored when goal setting with learners/colleagues?

✓ To do list

- ☐ Review your existing target-setting processes in the light of your reading.
- ☐ Introduce your learners to Olympic goal setting and encourage them to utilize it.
- ☐ Have your learners record targets somewhere centrally.
- ☐ Teach your learners to use the timeline process and get them to use it for complex or multiple targets.
- ☐ Use the processes described here for your own targets.

Want to find out more?

Persuad, R. (2006) *The Motivated Mind*. Bantam Press.

James, T. (1988) *Timeline Therapy and the Basis of Personality*. Meta Publications.

McKenna, P. & Maister, D. (2002) *First Among Equals*. Free Press.

See also . . .

→❖ Accelerated learning, page 5.

→❖ Managing learners' behaviour, page 95.

→❖ Personalization in education, page 146.

→❖ Underachievement, page 192.

46

Teaching style

What is it?

Your *teaching style* is the overall flavour of your teaching methods and approaches at any moment in time. It includes such things as your use of space in the classroom, your language and the manner in which you ask questions, your persona and the type of responses you seek from learners. Taken together, it adds up to the classroom climate you create for your learners.

Knowledge bank

- Most learners enjoy a *variety* of teaching styles throughout their day and in your lesson there are many opportunities for offering different teaching styles.
- Though it can vary according to the content of the lesson and learning tasks, most teachers tend to have a *dominant* or preferred teaching style – their 'default position' which learners come to recognize.

- Your teaching style has a very significant bearing on learning because it tends to affect the ability of learners with different →✢ **learning preferences** (page 86) from accessing the learning. For example, if you always teach through visual approaches, then learners who enjoy auditory or kinaesthetic approaches may feel excluded.

- Through your first few years as a teacher it's likely that your teaching style will vary quite a bit before things start to stabilize and routines begin to become embedded.

- Perhaps the worse-case scenario is for your learners to become habituated to your predominant teaching style so that it no longer engages them. In such situations learners can begin to switch off because your teaching becomes part of the fabric of their classroom rather than a dynamic human interaction requiring their involvement.

- The box opposite describes three teaching styles that help to illustrate the scope of what is possible, while also indicating the learning preferences that each approach appeals most to.

- It is, however, important not to view teaching and learning style as an equation to be maximized: there is no one type of teaching that suits one type of learner all the time. Variety and flexibility are important for both teachers and learners.

- The teaching of certain subjects often lends itself to a particular style, for example in English there is frequently a performance element that complements the teaching of some content, and in science the emphasis of practical lessons is on 'doing'. However, this should not be taken for an excuse to *always* teach in these ways.

- The key message about teaching style is *fitness for purpose* – all teachers should try to develop a repertoire of teaching styles in order to help learners to learn in diverse ways, according to the learning outcomes in hand. It is certainly not a case of teachers adopting one type of teaching style all the time.

The performer

This teaching style is highly dynamic and involves the teacher in entertaining learners through a highly theatrical approach. This may involve the teacher taking the role of a famous character or moving swiftly through the classroom in an animated way in order to get points across. When successful this teaching style often results in much laughter from learners and a sense of fun being injected into learning. Learners with visual and auditory learning preferences tend to find this teaching style appealing.

The doer

Learners in a classroom where this teaching style is used tend to be encouraged by the teacher to 'get on and do' things. The teacher using this teaching style will often start the lesson off in a highly practical way, showing how learners themselves can get 'hands-on' in their learning. Throughout the classroom there are examples of learners' work and the teacher tries to cultivate a busy atmosphere, with frequent reminders of how much time is left in the lesson. Learners with a kinaesthetic learning preference tend to find this teaching style attractive.

The reflector

Learners who have a preference for inter- and intra-personal matters tend to enjoy a teaching style typified by reflection. Here, the teacher encourages learners to consider the big picture, discuss how things were done and why they were done this way. There is a value placed on the discussion of feelings and motivations in such a classroom and learners are often invited to review their own work to learn the lessons for next time. As much time seems to be devoted to looking back over work done as looking forward towards what will be done next.

Ask yourself

1 Consider a great teacher you had at school and one that was not so effective – what were their teaching styles like? What specific aspects of their styles appealed to you, or failed to engage?

2 What is your dominant teaching style? How would learners in your classroom describe you as a teacher?

3 Which learning preferences does your teaching style encourage? Which are in danger of being ignored?

✔ To do list

☐ Ask somebody to observe your lesson in order to record your teaching style and how it varies during the lesson. Better still, get them to film you as you teach so you have a record to refer back to.

☐ Open a dialogue with your learners about teaching style and what their preferences are – this can often reveal important information about them as learners, as well as you as a teacher. Consider issuing questionnaires to seek learners' views more systematically.

☐ Observe others teach with the specific aim of learning more about the teaching style of your colleagues. Consider which features of their teaching styles you would like to mirror in your classroom.

Want to find out more?

Despite its importance, teaching style has not been the subject of many education books. Several software companies offer products which enable you to analyse your teaching style in detail, with one of the most popular being Teaching Style Analysis (www.creativelearningcentre.com). The following book has a more detailed discussion of teaching styles than most – Petty, G. (2004) *Teaching Today*. Nelson Thornes.

See also . . .

→✣ Differentiation, page 38.
→✣ Learning preferences, page 86.
→✣ Managing learners' behaviour, page 95.
→✣ Personalization in education, page 146.
→✣ Questioning, page 155.

47

Thinking skills

What are they?

Thinking skills are skills which promote reflection and more incisive thinking, enabling learners to know 'how' as well as 'what'. They help learners to learn how to learn. *Metacognition* is the process of 'thinking about thinking', reflecting on the thinking process at work so that it can be analysed and effective approaches identified.

Knowledge bank

- The important place of thinking skills in UK schools today is thanks to the work of a number of key figures since the 1940s.
- The major pioneers in developing thinking skills were psychologist Reuven Feuerstein and philosopher Matthew Lipman.
- Feuerstein worked in Israel after World War II with traumatized young Jews who flooded into the country, developing a set of

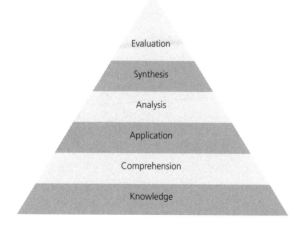

Bloom's taxonomy

cognitive interventions called '*instrumental enrichment*', which helped them to learn more effectively.

- Lipman worked with university students in the USA to help them to think for themselves, eventually producing materials of key relevance for schools under the auspices of the Institute for the Advancement of Philosophy for Children.
- Maltese thinker Edward de Bono contributed much to the debate on thinking skills during the 1970s and 1980s, especially through his concept of lateral thinking and specific techniques to promote more effective thinking (e.g. six hats approach).
- Another important reference point for teachers interested in thinking skills is the work of Benjamin Bloom. In the 1950s he developed a 'taxonomy of cognitive development' which still has resonance in UK schools today.
- Whether intended or not, Bloom's taxonomy has led teachers to talk about a 'hierarchy' of thinking skills, with those at the base of Bloom's pyramid deemed 'lower-order thinking skills' and those towards the top 'higher-order skills'. Many teachers have been eager to help their learners to develop higher-order thinking skills as these are seen as more valuable for solving complex problems, making difficult decisions or carrying out high-quality work.

- In the UK pivotal work on thinking skills was carried out in the 1980s by a research team from King's College, London, led by Philip Adey and Michael Shayer. They developed an intervention strategy for science teaching in years 7 and 8 called Cognitive Acceleration through Science Education (CASE; →✢ **Cognitive acceleration programmes**, page 24).

- In the late 1990s UK government interest in thinking skills gathered pace and Professor Carol McGuinness from Queen's University, Belfast, carried out an important review on their effectiveness in improving educational standards. This was followed by their inclusion in the new Key Stage 3 Strategy published shortly afterwards.

- There's been a big growth in interest in thinking skills in recent years in UK schools as many teachers have come to realize that they are a much neglected, but vitally important, part of any curriculum.

- Thinking skills are not, of course, a new approach, but the advent of the National Curriculum has allowed their importance to become buried among a mass of content. The National Curriculum contains 352 pages detailing the knowledge and skills required of young people, but includes just four pages on thinking skills.

- The National Curriculum document states that 'thinking skills complement the key skills [of communication, application of number, information technology, working with others, improving own learning and performance, and problem solving] and are embedded in the National Curriculum'.

- Five core thinking skills are included in the National Curriculum as shown in the table overleaf.

- By trying to develop learners' thinking skills, teachers are able to develop so-called 'communities of enquiry' through the use of carefully structured dialogue. By doing this they can help to develop an appreciation of the value of *metacognition*.

- Belle Wallace's Thinking Actively in a Social Context (TASC) approach combines many of the best elements of thinking skills approaches, rolled together into an easy to follow all-embracing framework for learning and problem-solving.

Information-processing skills	These enable learners to: – locate and collect relevant information – sort, classify, sequence, compare and contrast – analyse part/whole relationships
Reasoning skills	These enable learners to: – give reasons for opinions and actions – draw inferences and make deductions – use precise language to explain what they think – make judgements and decisions informed by reasons or evidence
Enquiry skills	These enable learners to: – ask relevant questions – pose and define problems – plan what to do and how to research – predict outcomes and anticipate consequences – test conclusions and improve ideas
Creative thinking skills	These enable learners to: – generate and extend ideas – suggest hypotheses – apply imagination – look for alternative innovative outcomes
Evaluation skills	These enable learners to: – evaluate information – judge the value of what they read, hear and do – develop criteria for judging the value of their own and others' work or ideas – have confidence in their judgements

Core thinking skills

- More recently, tools and practical approaches to develop thinking skills have been developed, including the logovisual thinking (LVT) method.
- Effective teaching should combine work on thinking skills with the key subject content of any curriculum area – learners can't reach their full potential if either is neglected. Traditionally, teachers have been encouraged to value curriculum content over thinking skills, but the CASE programme, which covered less content than standard lessons yet enabled learners to achieve better results, provides sound evidence to back up a move away from heavy curriculum content.
- Bear in mind that there are thinking skills which may be quite specific to your subject area – do not fall into the trap of thinking, for example, that once a learner can analyse something in one lesson, they can transfer those analytical skills to another.

Ask yourself

1 To what extent do you develop your learners' thinking skills in their lessons and their homework?
2 What is the balance between work to develop your learners' lower- and higher-order thinking skills?
3 How would you describe your own thinking skills? Are there areas which need further development?

✓ To do list

☐ Try to widen your repertoire of techniques to develop thinking skills in your subject area, through studying some of the excellent texts now available (see below).

☐ Specific courses are now available that will enable you to fast track your skills in teaching thinking skills – find one that particularly interests you.

☐ Join with other interested teachers in your school to carry out some action research into the effects of introducing more work on thinking skills.

Want to find out more?

Adey, P. & Shayer, M. (1994) *Really Raising Standards: Cognitive Intervention And Academic Achievement.* Continuum.

De Bono, E. (1990) *Lateral Thinking: A Textbook of Creativity.* Penguin.

Fisher, R. (2003). *Teaching Thinking: Philosophical Enquiry in The Classroom.* Continuum.

McGuinness, C. (1999) *From Thinking Skills to Thinking Classrooms: A Review and Evaluation of Approaches for Developing Pupils' Thinking.* DFEE (Research Report RR115). Available online at www.dfes.gov.uk/research/data/uploadfiles/RB115.doc

Wallace, B. (2004) *Thinking Skills and Problem-solving: An Inclusive Approach.* NACE and David Fulton Publishers.

Chris Kington Publishing (www.chriskingtonpublishing.co.uk) is a leading educational publisher producing books that focus on thinking skills in specific curriculum areas, together with generic approaches such as logovisual thinking. Includes titles in the award-winning *Thinking through . . .* series.

Institute for the Advancement of Philosophy for Children (IAPC): http://cehs.montclair.edu/academic/iapc/

See also . . .

→❖ Cognitive acceleration programmes, page 24.

→❖ Constructivism, page 27.

→❖ Questioning, page 155.

48

Transition

What is it?

Transition is generally taken to mean the point at which a child transfers from one stage of their schooling to another. It is usually used to mean the change from primary to secondary education, however it must be remembered that in some areas there is a further tier in the system which means that a child undergoes two transition periods, from primary to middle and then from middle to high school.

Knowledge bank

- Transition to a new school results in a number of changes in the child's life, spanning social, personal and academic areas:
  - different routines – this could involve longer days, increased travel etc.
  - a wider peer group and therefore new friends and loss of contact time with established friends

- additional responsibilities and new activities
- a broader curriculum
- interaction with a larger number of staff — often the first encounter with subject specialist staff occurs at the transfer from primary to secondary school.

- It is often assumed that children transfer along with other members of their own year group – but it should be remembered that this is not always the case as sometimes a child will transfer to a new school *mid-way* through a term. For these youngsters this period can be doubly disturbing as they will be undergoing the same experiences but will also be doing so on their own. In certain cases, such as the children of service families or children in care, it may also be one of a series of transitions.

- Data collected by the National Foundation for Educational Research (NFER) has shown that 40 per cent of children lose motivation and stop making progress (in maths, English and science) in the year after transfer to secondary school. However, this is in relation to attainment measured according to National Curriculum levels and not standardized tests, so this should be treated with some caution. Equally, it must be remembered that the effect of dips in progress is not consistent across schools, subjects or individual learners. Nevertheless, this finding is in line with earlier studies and does suggest that there is a lack of progress in some key subjects.

- A 2005 Ofsted evaluation of the Secondary National Strategy suggested that the continuity of learning was judged unsatisfactory in nearly a quarter of schools visited, and information sharing was identified as a particular weakness. It suggests that improving the quality of information about learners' prior attainment is vital to ensuring effective transfer. Secondary schools can use the data to plan for progression in year 7, especially for those learners who have not achieved the expected levels at the end of Key Stage 2. The report argues that this will mean that the expectations of progress for each learner will then be challenging but realistic, and that teachers can use the information to avoid covering familiar ground.

- The research into transfer and transitions argues that learners respond most effectively to a *balance* between the familiar and the new. This applies to teaching styles as well as to content – while some learners may thrive on variety and change, others may find it overwhelming. Planned progression can ensure that learners are consistently challenged. However, schools should recognize learners' progress. As they mature, learners should be able to take increasing responsibility for themselves and for their learning.

- The variety of reasons for children experiencing difficulties with the transition from primary to secondary education has led to many schools adopting a multifaceted approach to the issues. This requires the improving of learners' pastoral experiences, in conjunction with smoothing out the cultural differences between the primary and secondary phases, where curriculum transfer is paramount. The responsibility for effective transition is best shared between the two schools involved to create a situation where there is a dual acceptance of responsibility. However, it is vitally important to involve children and their parents too. The White Paper ➙✤ *Every Child Matters* (page 53) supports this by stressing the need to put parents at the heart of decisions to improve each child's life chances.

- The Secondary National Strategy advises that teachers build on prior knowledge, introducing new learning styles when appropriate. A number of guidance documents have been produced to support improvement in transfer practices. These range from guidance for school leaders wishing to adopt a whole-school approach to improvement, to subject-specific work plans for teachers. Further information can be found on the DfES standards website.

  - It's vital that learners with special educational needs are encouraged to face the change with confidence and the secondary SEN coordinator should be working up to 12 months ahead. Close partnership is required between the schools to ensure that particular learning needs are anticipated and to allow the secondary school to develop learning plans that will maximize the opportunities of each child. A more gradual induction package is also useful as this will allow the learners to feel more at ease in the new environment and allow for further observation and assessment.

  - Increasing mobility in the population means that 'individual transition' (i.e. where one child moves to a new school without their peers) is an increasing trend, resulting in more learners finding themselves 'the new kid' in school. Often this change is accompanied by other changes such as alteration in family circumstances, such as parental separation. Moving is one of the most stressful life experiences and such changes can make children and young people feel particularly vulnerable. A change in school will also mean a change in peer group, structure, learning and interaction with adults beyond their family circle and for secondary students it may also include a change in syllabus with exam subjects. Faced with upheavals of this nature it's natural for a child to grieve over their 'lost' school and friendships. They may also struggle with fear of the unknown – and general insecurity – as the environment in which they came to feel secure has been stripped away. However, every move has positive aspects, with the potential for a fresh start, new possibilities and friendships.

- It is important that time is spent on resolving transition problems early, so that the child begins to feel confident in their new environment and doesn't feel that they have lost their identity. Often, the issues which arise might be practical considerations such as learning a new time-table or getting used to a different approach to work or new expectations. Other issues may relate to establishing friendship groups. It's useful to provide a 'buddy' system to ensure that there's a one-to-one induction process. For learners involved in individual transition, it's best if the newcomer can start at the beginning of a new term or after a half-term in order to aid integration. Adequate, open and honest dialogue with parents is essential so that they can highlight any possible areas of need.

- Primary schools can also help with children who leave by taking steps to ease the transition. The prompt reply to the new school and sending on of transfer information can assist everyone and means that the child feels less adrift. Encourage children to also take examples of their work to the new school and where appropriate retain some kind of contact so that individuals do not feel totally isolated in the early stage of transfer. By ensuring that the new school receives as much information as possible about the child's achievements to date, and the stage they are at in their learning, the chance of the student being given work at an inappropriate level will be reduced.

Transition tips for secondary schools

1 *Involve parents* – ensure that they feel part of the change-over process. Visit feeder schools to hold events to inform them about curricular and extra-curricular activities. Ensure that they feel they can visit the secondary school and have opportunities to become part of school life.

2 *Transition booklets* – an informal profile listing, not just academic strengths and weaknesses but also information about likes and dislikes.

3 *Interactive website* – this should be aimed at the new intake with items such as virtual tours, activities which link to work done in year 6 and a chance to find out more about the school.

4 *Teacher link* – build in ways for staff from your school to visit feeder schools on a rota basis to take some classes (e.g. science, art, music, PE). This allows staff and students to get to know one another.

5 *Transition work units* – particularly useful in core subjects. A unit is planned which can be started in the primaries in the summer term and then completed in the first week of September in the new secondary. It is also useful, where possible, to use materials which link or match with those used in the feeder schools to ensure that there is a uniformity of background information.

6 *Video lessons* – staff from the secondary and feeder primaries video lessons for one another to watch to highlight any significant differences in approach, and work towards ensuring consistency.

7 *Use former students* – the pastoral team and transition co-ordinator meet small groups of students to discuss fears and misconceptions, along with students from the previous year group from the individual feeder schools.

8 *Involve children in planning* – year 6 children complete questionnaire confidentially about what they like about school and any areas they find difficult. They also choose two friends who they would like to be with in their new tutor group and have the opportunity to mention anyone they particularly would wish to avoid.

9 *Hold a summer school* – a short activity school (e.g. three days) aimed particularly at students who have been flagged up as being likely to be of concern, or needing longer to familiarize themselves with the new school (perhaps those who seem to be at risk of being isolated).

10 *Safe haven* – ensure that there's a special social area specifically for year 7 use to prevent them feeling overwhelmed (e.g. a special playground).

11 *First day* – ensure that the first day of the new school year is exclusively for year 7, so that they can learn to find their way around without being swamped by larger students. Incorporate activities such as a treasure hunt which involves them finding their way to specific areas in pairs or small groups.

12 *And the good news . . .* – each student has a book given to them during the first week of term in which they write down the good news about what has happened to them each week, as well as any bad news or particular concerns. This encourages positive reflection as well as allowing a confidential way of informing tutors of any issues. The books are read by their tutor and any 'bad news' dealt with before end of school each Friday, in order to prevent anxieties growing over the weekend.

Ask yourself

1 To what extent does transition have implications for the subject(s) you teach?

2 How do you cater for the effects of transition in your teaching?

3 How do your learners appear to be affected by this issue?

4 How could you improve the transition experience for your learners?

5 What barriers might you face in working in this and how might they be overcome?

✓ To do list

☐ Find out more about the transition procedures underway in your school.

☐ Decide on three aspects of transition that you can assist with through specific actions in your classroom.

☐ Work with a like-minded colleague to explore more widely how your classroom practice can ease transition, especially for learners who are vulnerable.

Want to find out more?

Transfer and Transitions in the Middle Years of Schooling (7–14): Continuities and Discontinuities in Learning is available from the DfES website at www.dfes.gov.uk.

Curriculum Continuity: Effective Transfer Between Primary and Secondary Schools is available from www.standards.dfes.gov.uk/ keystage3

www.dfes.gov.uk /findoutmore.dfes.gov.uk/2006/08/ from_primary_to.html

See also . . .

→❖ National Strategies for schools, page 133.

→❖ Personalization in education, page 146.

49

Underachievement

What is it?

Underachievement occurs when learners do not reach their expected level of performance in one or more aspects of school life. Though often judged in terms of academic success and test or examination results, underachievement also encompasses 'softer' measures such as interpersonal skills and the ability to manage one's own behaviour.

Knowledge bank

- Underachievement has been hi-jacked by the government as a rod with which to beat 'failing' schools, but [avoiding] it should be central to the mission of *all* schools. Every school must do what it can to ensure that no learner is disadvantaged in life by failing to reach his or her potential.
- Sophisticated statistical measures have been devised to help teachers to determine whether learners are underachieving in

specific areas – chiefly those which are deemed to be important by the government.

- The 'softer' aspects of underachievement have received less attention, perhaps because they are more difficult to measure – but they are no less important.

- Work at the school or subject level often reveals that particular groups of learners are underachieving more than others – such as boys, more able learners or those with a particular disability. This enables measures to be introduced in order to address the needs of a whole cohort of learners.

- A multiplicity of reasons may lie behind any individual's underachievement, combining both factors from outside school and things that are under your control within your establishment.

- Over the last few years there has been a lot of work to investigate and address the underachievement of boys and this area has been the subject of much additional government funding and projects.

- Controversy has surrounded the subject of underachievement, because not everyone agrees about the measures that can be used to judge whether an individual is underachieving. In particular, the need for a reliable baseline against which to judge whether future achievement is in line with expectations, is paramount.

Ask yourself

1 Which aspects of underachievement are most important to you? What about your school's leaders and the government?

2 What measures are in place in your school to identify, track and address underachievement?

3 How can you measure the aspects of underachievement that are most important to you?

✓ To do list

☐ Find out whether there are any specific initiatives underway in your school or local authority to target underachievement.

194 **Everything You Need to Know About Teaching**

☐ Focusing on three learners in a class you currently teach, consider their achievement in detail and prepare a mini profile for each, outlining in which areas they may be underachieving. Then devise an action plan to address this.

☐ Encourage your learners to talk to you openly about what they find difficult or challenging – the reasons for their underachievement sometimes lie in these specific difficulties, which are not always obvious to the teacher.

Want to find out more?

Jha, J. (2007) *Boys' Underachievement in Education.* Commonwealth Secretariat.

Smith, E. (2007) *Analysing Underachievement in Schools.* Continuum International Publishing.

West, A. & Pennell, H. (2003) *Underachievement in Schools.* Routledge Falmer.

See also . . .

→✢ Differentiation, page 38.
→✢ Inclusion, page 78.
→✢ Managing learners' behaviour, page 95.
→✢ Mentoring, page 110.
→✢ Personalization in education, page 146.

50

Writing frames/ scaffolding

What are they?

A *writing frame*, or scaffold, is a means whereby learners are assisted to develop the independent skills necessary for different types of writing. The process of enabling learners to develop more effective writing through the use of such tools is often called *scaffolding*, but this can also convey the wider sense of providing specific types of support to enable learners to progress.

Knowledge bank

- Writing frames can include both written and visual prompts and can be used in a variety of ways within the Literacy Hour, or within specialist subjects in groups, full class or as paired or individual prompts, by being tailored to meet the specific needs of different learners. They provide a means by which the learner can gather their thoughts, organize them and then provide a framework for recording ideas.

- Within subject specialisms the use of a frame means that the learner is able to concentrate on what they want to say, rather than get confused by the actual form. However, a frame or scaffold can also be used to familiarize a learner with different types of writing, so that they can then learn to use the most appropriate format for the task.

- A writing frame is most effective when it is used in a way that encourages learners to *extend* their repertoire of writing genres. They can assist with the learning of more formal registers, while also improving the overall cohesiveness of learners' writing. This encourages learners to tackle different writing tasks independently in their own lives.

- In order to achieve this level of effectiveness a writing frame should offer sufficient *support* to help the learner attempt a new or difficult task, but without providing so much guidance that the writing is reduced to filling in boxes. This does not leave sufficient scope for the writer to improve and become independent. It's important to always bear in mind that the ultimate aim of the frame is to assist the writer to produce *independent continuous text*, at the appropriate level.

- Frames should always be designed and used *progressively* so that less scaffolding should be required for more difficult tasks as the learners gain experience and skills.

- The effectiveness of frames increases if they are used as part of the planning and drafting stages, as this helps learners to marshal their thoughts and organize what they want to write.

- It's also important to remember that learners need to be shown how to use the frame in order to shape their ideas and for this reason it's often useful to introduce the idea of 'scaffolded writing', by presenting an opportunity for a class to develop a writing frame together. This allows the learners to see how a frame is formed and how following the frame can help them to write with purpose.

- A frame should always be structured to suit the type of text and style of writing being practised. The amount of detail required in a writing frame can vary enormously depending on the purpose of the frame.

  - A frame for writing explanatory information text would require headings, subheadings and suggestions for connectives to link the paragraphs.

- A frame for writing a letter would require an example of the correct layout, suggestions for opening salutations, opening sentence and appropriate closure suggestions.
- Writing requiring the presentation of an argument would require suggestions for sentence openings for presenting contrasting points of view.
- Technical writing, such as recipes or the writing up of experiments, would require examples of format and appropriate language.

• A danger already highlighted is that it is only too easy to lose sight of the idea that using writing frames should be progressive. As a learner gains in confidence, so the frames ideally should be designed to encourage independent writing. Unfortunately, it can very easily become the case that the framework actually becomes a strait-jacket which stifles independent thought.

• A good frame should allow scope for development. In situations that require creative thinking – such as story-writing – a frame may very swiftly become overly prescriptive and so be counter-productive. At their worst a frame can foster the 'and then' syndrome and the structure provided by the frame may be viewed by the learner as being fixed and unchangeable. This in itself can lead to an over-reliance on the frame as it is seen as being 'the right answer' and therefore the only answer. In order to prevent this it must always be remembered that the use of writing frames should only form *part* of a learner's writing experiences in any subject.

• ICT can be used to create writing frames that allow learners to compose directly onto a screen or a shared whiteboard. This has the additional advantage of the enlarged format being available for use in class for collaborative work. Individuals can also work directly on to a screen by inserting typed, scanned or pasted material. It is important, however, when developing screen-based writing frames to allow sufficient space for learners to develop their ideas without losing sight of the big picture. New text moves the frames further down the screen and this can lead to learners losing the idea of continuity in the planning of their work.

• A number of writing frames are already available online as resources for teachers, from the usual teaching websites as well as those listed below. They include both literacy-based frames and subject-specialist frames. However, as with all external sources it's important to remember that they will require study and possibly adaptation prior to use.

- Learning through *imitation* and observation, and teaching through *modelling,* are approaches that are having increasing resonance in schools. Socially, we often learn through imitation and by shifting the emphasis towards a collaborative social approach, the idea of scaffolding is one with which most children are familiar. In short, we learn how to do things by copying the way others do them. Imitation is, therefore, a natural way in which we learn how to construct new ideas.

Suggestions for using writing frames

1 A way of illustrating key structural features of a variety of writing genres.
2 To provide a structure and markers to help learners to order their ideas and written work.
3 To encourage learners to develop a range of sentence starters and connectives.
4 To practise the organizing of information into an appropriate format for writing.
5 Enlarged frames for teacher modelling and collaborative work in guided and independent sessions.
6 Provision of additional support for less confident writers by the provision of prompts.
7 Used in conjunction with a computer so that information can be typed, scanned, or cut and pasted with key words and phrases.

Ask yourself

1 To what extent do you use writing frames in the subject(s) you teach?
2 How do you currently use them?
3 What barriers exist to your own use and how might they be overcome?